CW00418187

WOMEN WRITERS OF THE
SEVENTEENTH CENTURY

W

WOMEN WRITERS OF THE SEVENTEENTH CENTURY

Ramona Wray

Northcote House
in association with the
British Council

© Copyright 2004 by Ramona Wray

First published in 2004 by Northcote House Publishers Ltd, Horndon, Tavistock, Devon, PL19 9NQ, United Kingdom.
Tel: +44 (01822) 810066. Fax: +44 (01822) 810034.

British Library Cataloguing-in-Publication Data
A catalogue record for this book is available from the British Library

ISBN 0-7463-1128-1 hardcover
ISBN 0-7463-0882-5 paperback

Typeset by TW Typesetting, Plymouth, Devon
Printed and bound in the United Kingdom by
Athenaeum Press Ltd., Gateshead, Tyne & Wear

Contents

Acknowledgements

I would like to thank Nicky Grene and Eiléan Ní Chuilleanáin who read earlier versions of some of these chapters and who offered invaluable comment. More broadly, both have always been generous with counsel and support.

Helen Wilcox and Suzanne Trill have also provided salient advice on how individual chapters could be improved – sometimes even without knowing it. Throughout the process of writing this book, and much else, Suzanne Trill has been an important source of energy, expertise and understanding. This study would be much the poorer without her.

I am also grateful to Isobel Armstrong for believing in this project, for timely guidance on how it could be achieved and for continuing encouragement. At Northcote House, Brian Hulme has been a model editor.

Mark Thornton Burnett has read the entire manuscript and made numerous suggestions for improvement – to him I am the most indebted.

Biographical Outlines

This book departs from the convention of other studies in the Writers and their Work series in that it does not concentrate on a single author. Its focus, rather, resides with a series of writers representative of women's writing during the seventeenth century. Accordingly, I have not elected to provide biographical outlines of all seventeenth-century female authors (such a task would be impossible within the present confines) but to offer brief histories of the seven writers upon which the study concentrates. As is evident below, each writer is attached to a particular chapter, and further biographical information about the writers will be found in the chapters themselves.

Elizabeth Cary, Lady Falkland (1585 or 1586–1639) – chapter 1

The daughter of an Oxfordshire lawyer and an expert in a number of European languages, Cary separated from her husband, Sir Henry Cary, in 1626 when she converted to the Catholic religion. Her works include *The Tragedy of Mariam* (1613), a Senecan translation, a biography of Tamburlaine and several lives of the saints. With the exception of the tragedy, these other works have been lost. Cary translated (but had publicly burned) *The Reply of the Most Illustrious Cardinal of Perron* (1630), and also produced a translation of Ortelius; a 1627 blank-verse history of Edward II has, likewise, been said to be her work. She was the recipient of several literary dedications, and one of her daughters, a nun, wrote a hagiographic account of her life.

Aemilia Lanyer (1569 or 1570–1645) – chapter 2

The daughter of Baptista Bassano, an Elizabethan court musician, Lanyer may have been employed in the household of the Countess of Kent as a young woman. She also seems to have been mistress to Henry Carey, Lord Hunsdon, the Lord Chamberlain. Pregnant by him in 1592, she was married to Alphonso Lanyer, and, finding herself in monetary difficulties soon afterwards, consulted Simon Forman, the astrologer. In later life, Lanyer owned a school and, in 1635, petitioned the courts for monies due to her from her ex-husband's monopolies. *Salve Deus Rex Judaeorum* (1611) is her only extant work.

Elizabeth Joscelin (1595 or 1596–1622) – chapter 3

Contrary to the views of her seventeenth-century editor, Elizabeth Joscelin's parents, Sir Richard Brooke and Joan Chaderton, seem to have separated during her lifetime. Educated by her maternal grandfather, Joscelin married Tourell Joscelin in 1616. While pregnant with her first child in 1622, Joscelin wrote *The Mother's Legacy to Her Unborn Child*. Her daughter, Theodora, was born on 12 October; nine days later, Joscelin died.

Anna Trapnel (*c.* 1622–?) – chapter 4

Trapnel was the daughter of a shipwright and appears to have been a member of the Fifth Monarchist movement from at least 1642 onwards. In 1645 and again in 1647, she worked as a house companion; also in 1647, she consulted the contemporary prophet, Sarah Wight. She travelled to Cornwall in 1654, spending a brief period in Bridewell as a result. Subsequently, she experienced the first of her many trances. From October 1657, she fell into a trance which lasted for a ten-month period. Trapnel wrote *The Cry of a Stone* (1654), *A Legacy for Saints* (1654), *Anna Trapnel's Report* (1654), *Strange and Wonderful News from Whitehall* (1654) and *A Voice for the King of Saints* (1658).

Mary Rich, Countess of Warwick (1625–78) – chapter 5

Daughter of Richard Boyle, the Earl of Cork, Mary Rich married in secret Charles Rich, a younger son. She composed a number of religious reflections and meditations, these being published in 1686. She also composed a memoir *c.* 1671 and kept a diary from 1666 to 1678.

Hannah Allen (*fl.* before 1670–83) – chapter 6

Little is known of Hannah Allen beyond the information provided in her conversion narrative, *Satan His Methods and Malice Baffled* (1683). From this we learn that she belonged to an Independent congregation, that she married Hannibal Allen and, after his death, Charles Hatt, and that she experienced periods of intense depression, leading to several suicide attempts.

Aphra Behn (*c.* 1640–89) – chapter 7

Aphra Behn may have been Aphra Johnson, born in Kent *c.* 1640. She enjoyed a gentlewoman's education and travelled, according to her own report, to Surinam in 1663–4. Returning to London, she probably married a merchant named Behn. He seems to have died from the plague in 1665. From 1665 onwards, she worked as a spy for the government in the Netherlands: 'Astraea' was her codename. Falling into debt in 1667, she returned to England, where she was briefly imprisoned. Despite offending Charles II in 1682, she conducted herself as an ardent Tory and Royalist. Her final days were plagued by illness and impoverishment. Behn was a prolific playwright, a distinguished poet, translator and prose fiction writer. She is notable for being the seventeenth century's first professional woman writer.

A Note on the Texts

There is no one standard authoritative edition of seventeenth-century women writers. Instead, the field is dominated by a number of different editions, which offer a useful, but not comprehensive, sense of the genres which female authors deployed and in which they participated. In the interests of accessibility, I have used such editions wherever possible. I would particularly recommend, for drama and poetry, two collections: S. P. Cerasano and Marion Wynne-Davies (eds), *Renaissance Drama by Women: Texts and Documents* (London and New York: Routledge, 1996) and Diane Purkiss (ed.), *Renaissance Women: The Plays of Elizabeth Cary/The Poems of Aemilia Lanyer* (London: Pickering, 1994). Also for poetry, these anthologies have proved particularly helpful: Germaine Greer, Susan Hastings, Jeslyn Medoff and Melinda Sansone (eds), *Kissing The Rod: An Anthology of Seventeenth-Century Women's Verse* (London: Virago, 1988) and Jane Stevenson and Peter Davidson (eds), *Early Modern Women Poets (1520–1700): An Anthology* (Oxford: Oxford University Press, 2001). Autobiographies are excellently extracted in Elspeth Graham, Hilary Hinds, Elaine Hobby and Helen Wilcox (eds), *Her Own Life: Autobiographical Writings by Seventeenth-Century Englishwomen* (London and New York: Routledge, 1989) and some diaries in Ralph Houlbrooke (ed.), *English Family Life, 1576–1716: An Anthology from Diaries* (Oxford: Blackwell, 1988). Mothers' advice books may be consulted in Sylvia Brown, (ed.), *Women's Writing in Stuart England: The Mothers' Legacies of Dorothy Leigh, Elizabeth Joscelin and Elizabeth Richardson* (Thrupp: Sutton, 1999). No edition of seventeenth-century women's prose fiction currently exists, although Book One of Lady Mary Wroth's

Urania appears in Paul Salzman (ed.), *An Anthology of Seventeenth-Century Fiction* (Oxford: Oxford University Press, 1991). There are also highly readable editions of individual seventeenth-century women writers, in which prose fiction features alongside other genres. Recommended here are Aphra Behn, *'Oroonoko', 'The Rover' and Other Works*, ed. Janet Todd (Harmondsworth: Penguin, 1992) and Margaret Cavendish, *'The Blazing World' and Other Writings*, ed. Kate Lilly (Harmondsworth: Penguin, 1992).

Elsewhere this book has availed itself of some older editions and compilations. Seventeenth-century editions are used where no reliable modern edition is available.

Where necessary, I have modernized quotations from seventeenth-century works.

Abbreviations

Full information about all the editions used may be found in the Notes and Bibliography. The following abbreviations, however, give an indication of those editions most frequently deployed.

A. Mary Rich, *Autobiography of Mary, Countess of Warwick*, ed. T. Croker (London: Percy Society, 1848)

CS Anna Trapnel, *The Cry of a Stone* (London, 1654; Wing T2031)

Grymeston Elizabeth Grymeston, *Miscellanea. Meditations. Memoratives* (London, 1604; S.T.C. 12407)

Joscelin Elizabeth Joscelin, *The Mother's Legacy to Her Unborn Child*, ed. Lord Bishop of Rochester (London and New York: Macmillan, 1894)

KR Germaine Greer, Susan Hastings, Jeslyn Medoff and Melinda Sansone (eds), *Kissing the Rod: An Anthology of Seventeenth-Century Women's Verse* (London: Virago, 1988)

M. Mary Rich, *Memoir of Lady Warwick: Also her Diary* (London: English Monthly Tract Society, 1847)

R. Anna Trapnel, *Anna Trapnel's Report* (London, 1654; Wing T2033)

S. Hannah Allen, *Satan His Methods and Malice Baffled* (London, 1683; Wing A1025)

WW Sylvia Brown (ed.), *Women's Writing in Stuart England: The Mothers' Legacies of Dorothy Leigh, Elizabeth Joscelin and Elizabeth Richardson* (Thrupp: Sutton, 1999)

Introduction

This book introduces readers to women's writings which span the breadth of the seventeenth century. In so doing, it traces the trajectory of women's writing from the first stirrings of female creativity in the late sixteenth century to the emergence of the fully fledged professional woman author at the Restoration. Across an expanse of one hundred years, *Women Writers of the Seventeenth Century* discovers women participating in many kinds of literary discourse, including drama, poetry, advice, prophecy, diaries, memoirs, conversion narratives and prose fiction. As a whole, the book argues that seventeenth-century women, despite living in a culture inimicable to the female literary endeavour, were able to take advantage of opportunities to appropriate, intervene in and, in some cases, radically transform their chosen textual fields. The effect of such experimentation, the argument suggests, was to allow some seventeenth-century women to create new idioms out of older vocabularies and to generate revitalized species of expression in the face of accepted patriarchal dictates.

By reaching beyond the familiar forms usually associated with seventeenth-century women's writing, this book underscores the urgency of attending to the material realities of female literary production. As Patricia Crawford's checklist of female works in print reveals, women's published writings in the seventeenth century mainly fall into religio-political categories.[1] That is, a majority of women exercise their voices through such mediums as the prose prophecy or the political pamphlet; these, of course, are unfamiliar types of literary expression with which modern readers may not be intimately acquainted. Perhaps because of the seeming inaccessibility

1

of these modalities, the dominant tendency among critics of early modern women's writing has been to concentrate upon more easily identifiable utterances (such as drama and poetry) and upon texts such as women's defences (these express sentiments which can easily be assimilated within a modern feminist consciousness).[2] Even inside the protection of traditional genres, the perspective has been skewed, with critics devoting disproportionate amounts of attention to poetry obeying a conventional format and passing over poetry produced in more radical manifestations. As a result, a panoply of vernacular configurations has slipped through the critical net, while criticism of traditional genres has simultaneously suffered, because texts have not been read in relation to the whole of women's literary output. In so far as literary genres can be precisely defined, this book reads established and more innovative materials side by side. Chapter 7, for example, which centres upon prose fiction, a form that has garnered generous doses of scrutiny, is juxtaposed with chapter 6's discussion of the conversion narrative. A type of autobiography, the conversion narrative attracted the greater numbers of women writers in the latter half of the century, yet it has so far escaped sustained investigation. The alignment is a felicitous one, since it permits a teasing out of the correspondences between two apparently separate representational vehicles while also pinpointing their contextual connections.

Insisting upon the importance of integrating an understanding of unfamiliar materials, *Women Writers of the Seventeenth Century* establishes the centrality of the Civil War period to a comprehensive assessment of women's literary industry. The once elided, middle years of the century take on a crucial significance in this book, not least because the revolutionary era was seminal for women's writing, producing the period's first great explosion of female-authored productions. But the Civil War was vital, too, in that the 1640s and the 1650s were responsible for precipitating the social, economic and political instabilities that, paradoxically, empowered women not only to conduct fresh generic explorations but also to assume privileged places at the heart of public life. Accordingly, chapter 4, which discusses the prophetic text, details the intriguing interdependencies between this sort of gendered articulation,

2

godly-approved statements and the shaping influence of seventeenth-century political upset.

In order to furnish both a general sense of women's writing activities and closer contextual adjudication, each chapter is divided into two parts. The first half of each chapter provides a descriptive account of the genre and sketches its development over the century's course, facilitating an engagement with the ways in which women intervened in peculiar genres at particular historical junctures. Such a procedure also enables a consideration of the possibilities, both formal and ideological, involved in the woman's inscription of herself within a discrete literary practice. Where necessary, the need for the modern interpreter to acquire new reading skills is highlighted. While some of the genres mapped in this book are self-evident – few readers, for example, need to be instructed in how to read poetry or drama – others are not. Those chapters dedicated to the prophecy and the conversion narrative invite the abandonment of inherited assumptions and encourage the development of alternative reading strategies; accordingly, the introductions to these parts of *Women Writers of the Seventeenth Century* are oriented towards the acquisition of a broader knowledge base and the refinement of existing applications. Nor does the need for the elaboration of a more nuanced understanding end with rarefied genres. Thus, chapter 5, which considers diaries and memoirs, makes a strong case for studying the period's distinctive autobiographical impulse through a particular lens, and finds virtue in placing alongside each other two orders of self-representation.

The complementary approaches adopted in the first half of each chapter are additionally reflective of the fact that different genres take on contrasting developmental complexions as the century progresses. In chapter 1, for example, it is seen that drama betrays a slow but inexorable movement away from translation and towards originality on the public stage. Other genres exhibit a steady regularity of form and purpose across the century's breadth; pertinent here are mothers' advice books, the cornerstone of chapter 3. In contradistinction again, some genres either are briefly illuminated, only to be quickly extinguished (relevant in this connection is chapter 6's engagement with the conversion narrative), or demonstrate variety and change throughout, eschewing any linear construction of progress (poetry, which is considered in chapter 2, is a case in point). Because poetry appears to follow no clearly signposted route through the seventeenth century, chapter 2 bases its debate on a recent anthology in order to survey a field resistant to straightforwardly temporal inquiry. The particular approach adapted in the chapter is appropriate for the singular intransigencies of its subject.

To illustrate the hypothesis that a unique positioning within a genre is specific to an individual woman writer, the second half of each chapter treats a single literary intervention as a case study. The case studies are not intended to be 'exemplary' or 'typical' of the genre; rather, they are elaborated as a series of local engagements, which are hardly representative of a complete narrative. Each case study pursues a practical example of the ways in which a woman's text creates a speaking position within a discrete discursive environment. These case studies work to point up differences among and between writers and genres, and are instrumental in suggesting the relative successes of female authors who appropriated literary traditions for their own purposes. The procedure also allows for a deeper appreciation of the range of classes, and religious and political affiliations, involved in the writing experience, while introducing questions about the links between generic choices and ideological allegiances. Why Mary Rich, Countess of Warwick, for example, chooses to write within the diary form, whereas Anna Trapnel, a shipwright's daughter, favours utilization of the prophetic text, is a creative line of inquiry. One explanation might be, as chapters 4 and 5 contend, that both writers appear at polar opposites in terms of their interpretive mechanisms and cultural locations.

Throughout, *Women Writers of the Seventeenth Century* argues for a close contextualization of female materials inside, on the one hand, social and historical trends and, on the other, a gendered reading of these determinants. The term 'writing woman' is now widely recognized as something of an oxymoron in seventeenth-century terms. Since contemporary women were frequently enjoined to silence in male-authored texts and exhorted to leave writing to their male counterparts, a useful aspect of any contextualizing procedure is the recognition of a masculinist culture averse to female authorship and, by extension, authority. All of the chapters in this book work within a logic that views the female voice as significant because it runs against the grain of the dominant antipathetic attitudes of its time. As part of an investment in contextualization, this book also conducts its investigations in line with recent reassessments of the female literary canon. In particular, it is responsive to the attempt to integrate women's manuscript work within a print tradition. Chapter 2 discusses the ways in which some contemporary women writers preferred to reach a more exclusive audience through the circulation of manuscript copies, and chapters 2, 3 and 5 rehearse examples of the distribution of these types of non-published material. By seeking, through selective attention, to assess a representative generic range as well as a variety of formats of transmission, *Women Writers of the Seventeenth Century* hopes to stimulate further inquiries and to redirect critical interest to the textual inceptions, and originary historical stimulations, of the period. In so doing, it makes a plea for the abiding resonance of the seventeenth-century female voice and for its undisputed critical centrality.

1

Drama

GENRE, RANGE, WRITERS

Over the course of the seventeenth century, plays by women grew in volume, scope and theatrical visibility. Drama throughout the early modern period was a male-dominated preserve, and thus it is not surprising that, during the sixteenth century, women tended to favour translation, a form of literary activity that asserted the primacy of the masculine classical text rather than the virtues of a female original composition. Known as 'closet dramas', these translations immediately declared the distance of women from an emergent public theatre. Produced by aristocratic women, 'closet dramas' were primarily designed to demonstrate the learning of their female translators, and, because not commercially performed, consigned the female voice to relative silence and anonymity. Yet, despite its seeming removal from the mainstream, the 'closet drama' could still be deployed to pass critical comment. For the spectacle of a woman sacrificed to facilitate political conflict in Lady Jane Lumley's *c.* 1550 translation of Euripedes' *Iphigenia at Aulis* formed an alliance with the situation of Lady Jane Grey, the ill-fated ten-day English queen. Similarly, the concern with the dangers of civil war, and the need for Roman rulers to respect their subjects, in the 1595 translation of Robert Garnier's *The Tragedy of Anthony* by Mary Sidney, the Countess of Pembroke, had, by the end of the sixteenth century, acquired a peculiarly topical Elizabethan urgency. These apparently private and restricted dramas by women, then, used the past to comment on contemporary affairs. In so doing, they opened up possibilities for gendered reflections upon the relationship

6

between women and the state in the same moment as they set the scene for more strident female interventions in the dramatic and political culture to come.

The seventeenth century witnessed the decline of the 'closet drama' genre and its gradual replacement by public forms of theatre in which professional women playwrights fully participated. At the same time, after Charles II's 1662 decree that parts previously performed by boys should now be taken by women, the theatre shifted in its ideological investments, becoming a space excitingly available to the female actress and artist. But this is not to imply that such a process was straightforward, or that women were to find in it a necessarily emancipatory experience. On the one hand, a rise in literacy permitted women from the middling sort, in ever greater numbers, both to have staged original dramas and to lay claim to a theatrical pre-eminence. In so doing, such women playwrights were to bring into the public domain the political insights first broached by their sixteenth-century predecessors. Moreover, the development of print technology during the seventeenth century encouraged many women playwrights, in an unprecedented fashion, to secure the publication of their work. The result was the appearance of a distinctively female dramatic culture, one characterized by its own conventions and preoccupations. On the other hand, the woman who pursued a theatrical career, whether as playwright or performer, was to find that access to public language was invariably attended, as Ros Ballaster states, 'by animadversions on her chastity'.[1] An equation between women, drama and prostitution was frequently on the lips of male detractors in the period, causing women to append strident defences of their professional conduct to their plays. (In this connection, it is perhaps understandable that 'closet drama' continued to attract some women, even if it was adopted for the commercial stage.) A further negative development was the separation, engineered by women playwrights themselves, between the writer and the actress, which suggests recurring points of contention rather than a sisterly solidarity. Certainly, then, women's drama underwent radical transformations during the seventeenth century; it would be a mistake, however, to maintain that these were uniform or that they consistently led in the direction of female empowerment.

Judged alongside these developments, *The Tragedy of Mariam* by Elizabeth Cary, Lady Falkland, which was composed *c.* 1603–4 and forms the case study for this chapter, occupies a singularly prescient place. First, it represents the earliest original composition by a female dramatist; secondly, the play was accorded in 1613 the permanency of print, a mark of the esteem in which the author was held. Almost certainly read aloud by Cary's domestic circle rather than performed as part of an aristocratic entertainment, *The Tragedy of Mariam* is no less distinctive for making available a multivalent female perspective. For, although centred upon the public ambitions of woman in the context of a repressive marriage, the play divides its sympathies unevenly between the female protagonists. Mariam, the Queen of Jewry, is constructed as combining arrogance and integrity in an ultimately Christ-like evocation of martyrdom. By contrast, it is Salome, the archetypal temptress, who exceeds Mariam's brand of passive resistance and argues for the woman's right to divorce. Whichever character is privileged, it is clear that *The Tragedy of Mariam* coheres around the conviction that patriarchy, an inherently unstable institution, is comprehensively incapable of defining the female subject.

If *The Tragedy of Mariam* is the first female-authored tragedy, *Love's Victory*, written by Lady Mary Wroth *c.* 1620, represents the first original comedy. Encouraged, no doubt, by her distinguished family – her uncle was Sir Philip Sidney and her aunt Mary Sidney, the Countess of Pembroke – Wroth gravitated easily to literary pursuits; more striking, however, is the fact that she manipulated her chosen genres to reflect upon personal circumstances. An unhappy marriage culminated in the death of her husband in 1616, after which Wroth commenced an extended affair with William Herbert, her cousin, only to be exiled from court as a result. These are the experiences underpinning *Love's Victory*, a play read or acted in a family circle and embracing characters that betoken 'real' people: the idealized lovers may indicate Wroth and Herbert, whereas the deceased husband is more akin to the uncultivated rustic. Such a bold, quasi-autobiographical brand of dramaturgy demanded a correspondingly innovative use of genre, and *Love's Victory* is further distinguished by its imaginative adaptation of a male-dominated form, pastoral tragicomedy.

Both *The Tragedy of Mariam* and *Love's Victory* are exceptional in design, range and implication. Yet, given their isolated status in the plethora of plays produced by men, it is difficult to detect in them overarching trends or preoccupations. Only with the expansion of women's drama in the later seventeenth century could clearly enunciated clusters of female-oriented interests be identified. Before that development, during the Interregnum, dramatic activity as a whole went underground in the wake of the official closure of the theatres. The Civil War had a doubled effect on dramatic writing by women. At once, its impact was to force women even further into the domestic interior, since political conflict precluded the possibility of mobility and/or professional exposure. Simultaneously, however, the larger divisions generated by the displacement of father figures in a nation-state at odds with itself were paradoxically enabling. Composed in 1643–5 by Lady Jane Cavendish and Lady Elizabeth Brackley, sisters imprisoned in the family castle at Bolsover, *The Concealed Fancies* is a case in point. This pastoral comedy features two sisters who, in the absence of a patriarch and confronted by a siege, accept their male suitors only after a newly egalitarian marital dispensation has been decided: the play is distinguished, then, by its privileging of male–female negotiation and its destabilizing perspective on sexual politics. Other plays of the period were indebted in comparable ways to a Civil War context. Margaret Cavendish, Duchess of Newcastle, whose plays were written in the 1650s, reformulated the historical narratives of the mid seventeenth century from her own vantage point. Her *Bell in Campo* (published 1662) concentrates on the exploits of Lady Victoria, who, in opposition to the tenets of masculinist martial exclusion, forms an army of Amazonian women, stuns with rhetorical bravura and secures royally approved domestic rights. A typical Cavendish heroine, Lady Victoria functions to question contemporary notions of women's 'natural' inferiority and impresses, in Karen Raber's words, with a scintillating combination of 'active virtue and aggressive honour'.[2] Immediately obvious in these plays is the extent of Royalist family connections. Lady Jane Cavendish and Lady Elizabeth Brackley were the stepdaughters of Margaret Cavendish, Duchess of Newcastle, women who, because of a communal material bond of dispossession and exile, were prompted to explore fresh avenues of theatrical practice. One consequence was a renewed attention to performance: although Margaret Cavendish's plays were not designed to be acted, being confined to the theatre of her own imagination, *The Concealed Fancies* almost certainly was, as its elaborate directions and machinery demonstrate. An additional by-product of the period's political vicissitudes was that moment of brief equality shared by men and women as dramatic practitioners: with all playwrights forced onto a similar footing, licence was allowed to conceive of the playmaking enterprise without reference to conventional institutional requirements.

Indeed, it is possible to argue that women's broader experimentation with drama during the Civil War was a condition for the opening out of the institution to female playwrights at the Restoration. Once theatres, in 1660, had unlocked their doors, an influx of professional women dramatists came to public notice. A survey of women's drama produced at this time clarifies that it runs the whole gamut of female representation. At one extreme are the plays of Frances Boothby and 'Ariadne' who, in *Marcelia* (1669) and *She Ventures and He Wins* (1695) respectively, depict proactive and self-determined women either challenging processes of male objectification or manipulating masculine adversaries to secure social and financial advantage. At the other extreme can be found more conservatively entrenched constructions of woman: Delarivier Manley's *The Royal Mischief* (1696), for example, discovers an unruly state, figured through equally riotous women, being contained through absolutist government, while Mary Pix's *Ibrahim* (1696) investigates the situation of demonic women who agitate to lead the head of state astray. But these dramatists did not subscribe only to polar positions. Nor did other playwrights necessarily take up predictable perspectives, preferring instead to concentrate on plotlines involving gender

10

inversion and disguise and even forms of dissident sexuality. Pertinent here is Catherine Trotter's play *Agnes de Castro* (1695), which is unique for dramatizing the virtues of love between women. A radical sexual agenda, as contemporary women's drama reveals, can also convey an interrogative political philosophy. In fact, a keen sensitivity to the ebb and flow of political life is a hallmark of more than one play of the period. Thus Katherine Philips' *Pompey* (1663) and *Horace* (1668), concerned, as they are, with the frustrations of female protagonists pincered between familial obligations and state loyalties, must have held a peculiar appeal to a court labouring in the shadow of the Civil War and endeavouring to resolve factions and heal divisions. More strident in political terms is Elizabeth Polwhele's tragedy, *The Faithful Virgins* (c. 1669–70), which, in the formulation of Alison Findlay and Stephanie Hodgson-Wright, 'adopts a high moral tone to criticize royal lust and sympathize with the isolation' of Catherine of Braganza, Charles II's 'slighted queen'.[3] If the type of woman delineated in later seventeenth-century drama is subject to flux and variation, then, so too is the political vision which the plays communicate and through which they are constituted.

The possibility of a woman's sexuality being seen in political terms was the product of a historical juncture marked by rapid developments at every level of the social fabric. Within the period, drama shaped and was shaped by changing conceptions of woman in a capitalist economy as well as by alarming swings in the country's equilibrium – the 'Popish Plot', the emergence of a two-party (Whig and Tory) system, religious dissent and the participation of the monarchy in, followed by their withdrawal from, popular theatrical entertainment. Always a yardstick of its moment, the theatre itself was judged simultaneously as a hive of iniquity and as a 'sentimental' forum for the 'reformation of manners'. Among women dramatists, it was Aphra Behn who registered the pulse of the times with the most insistent regularity and pronounced theatrical responsiveness. Behn dominated the theatrical scene from 1671 to 1689, with fifteen of her plays being printed and produced during these years. In and of herself Behn was a slippery dramatic phenomenon. A commitment to free love went hand in hand with an unflinching stress upon chastity;

approval of patriarchal Royalism sat uncomfortably next to the effort to privilege individual female agency; and woman-centred aspirations, as delineated in Behn's prefaces and prologues, did not invariably square with the content of the plays. These discontinuities aside, one impulse clearly stands out; as W. R. Owens and Lizbeth Goodman state: 'If writing is to be defined as male, [Behn] claims a "masculine part", and demands the opportunity not just to write for money, but to seek fame and her rightful place in the public literary tradition'.[4] Of her plays, *The Rover*, which was written in 1677, offers a particularly resonant summation of Behn's concerns. Centred upon the plight of a group of banished cavaliers, the play highlights, through its male–female courtships and rivalries, an equation between marriage and prostitution, a criticism of oppressive social institutions (such as arranged marriages) and a favourable construction of women as independent, desiring subjects. Yet the drama does not seamlessly incorporate all of its multiple elements, for, in the final scene, the former prostitute, Angelica Bianca, is excluded from the concluding unions. This might be understood as Behn's implicit arraignment of a double standard that both eulogizes and condemns female sexuality, but it indicates, too, I think, a submission to a male-defined ideological conundrum that the dramatist was unable properly to explicate.

By the end of the seventeenth century, therefore, women's drama had made prodigious strides from its private beginnings in 'closet' translations to its public incarnation in a larger theatrical setting. One might also suggest that this revolution in female playing and playmaking entailed a new recognition of women as producers and artists of important theatrical work. Certainly, from the perspective of twentieth- and twenty-first-century practice, drama by women of the seventeenth century is often ranked alongside the work of their male counterparts. There have been notable productions, for instance, of Behn's *The Lucky Chance* (1686) by the Women's Playhouse Trust in 1984, and of *The Rover* by the Royal Shakespeare Company in 1986 and again by the Women's Playhouse Trust in 1994. That these productions can now take place on such a regular basis is indication enough of the salient messages inscribed in seventeenth-century women's writing, and of the continuing relevancies this body of work contains for a modern sensibility.

CASE STUDY: ELIZABETH CARY, LADY FALKLAND, *THE TRAGEDY OF MARIAM* (1613)

As a case study for an opening chapter, Elizabeth Cary's *The Tragedy of Mariam* has much to offer. This is not only because the play is positioned on the cusp of the seventeenth century (composed *c.* 1603–4, it was not published until 1613), but because it exemplifies and elaborates two of the main restrictions imposed upon contemporary women – the twin doctrines of silence and chastity. The drama is notable for steering a skilful course between an idealization of these values and a suggestive deconstruction of their relevance to the female experience. Typical of the genre of 'closet drama', the play comprises a tragedy of state, focusing on the difficulty of maintaining individual integrity when faced with a repressive, tyrannous authority. Familiar, too, is the way in which questions of authority are addressed within both the public world and the private sphere, to the extent that political and domestic ramifications are seen to be intimately interlinked. Hence Herod is understood in Cary's dramaturgy to function simultaneously as monarch and husband, while Mariam is positioned at one and the same time as wife and subject.

The play commences in a carnivalesque space, one that has been opened up by Herod's supposed permanent absence from Judea (he is thought to have been executed). As a result of the removal of the play's political and patriarchal centre, opportunities for an alternative discursive register are facilitated. Appropriately enough, the opening soliloquy immediately directs attention to the theme of the female voice. Conflating the proverbially separate worlds of sexual and state politics, Mariam demands:

> How oft have I with public voice run on,
> To censure Rome's last hero for deceit
> . . . .
>
> But now I do recant and Roman lord
> Excuse, too rash a judgement in a woman,
> My sex pleads pardon . . .[5]

Mariam constructs herself as one used to speaking at length and in public on no less a subject than the political government of the nation. And, in condemning herself for doing so, she centres an audience's interests upon her gendered status as a woman. From the inception of the play, then, the female voice is tied to ideas of censure. In other scenes an embodiment of the chaste, beautiful and moral woman, Mariam here, and more generally, is discovered in terms of her loquaciousness. This talkative quality is the primary characteristic that distinguishes her from the play's remaining female characters. Thus, Salome, her sister-in-law and sworn enemy, describes her as 'the tongue that is . . . quickly moved' (I, 227), while Sohemus, the servant who regards Mariam so highly that he risks disobeying Herod to save her life, posits 'Unbridled speech' as the queen's 'worst disgrace' (III, 183). Friends and foes alike come together to arraign Mariam for a talk that is branded inordinate and a mode of speech that goes beyond prescribed perimeters.

Such a condemnation of Mariam makes sense only within a particular cultural logic that views public speech in gendered terms. The chorus develops the idea, arguing that a woman 'usurps upon another's right, / That seeks to be by public language graced' (III, 239–40) and establishing the right to public speech as an exclusively masculine privilege. But the play goes further than merely introducing gendered distinctions at the level of language. It explicitly teases out a cultural connection between silence and virtue that makes female speech not only an unfeminine but also a dangerously volatile enterprise. The chorus warns:

> That wife her hand against her fame doth rear
> That more than to her lord alone will give
> A private word to any second ear;
> And though she may with reputation live,
> Yet though most chaste, she doth her glory blot,
> And wounds her honour . . .
>
> (III, 227–32)

Speech directed at any other than a husband is here represented as calling into question the chastity of the woman involved: an unlicensed word, at the very least, signifies a blot on a presumably honourable reputation. The chorus' declaration makes clear that the female voice is linked to a loss of chastity; that is, the act of speaking is allied with the sexual act, and the practice of talking is judged akin to adultery. The chorus elaborates the train of associations:

> And though her thoughts reflect with purest light,
> Her mind if not peculiar is not chaste.
> For in a wife it is no worse to find,
> A common body, than a common mind.

(III, 241–4)

The 'reality' of what unfolds in a woman's mind is now seen to take second place to what takes place about her lips. Indeed, the two are equated and viewed as co-dependent. A comparable equation is later crucial to Herod's interpretation of Mariam's imputed infidelity. He becomes convinced that adultery has transpired only when he is assured that his wife's speech has been inappropriate; as he states: "'tis so. She's unchaste; / Her mouth will open to every stranger's ear' (IV, 432–3). At this point, Herod equates the opening of the female mouth with a scandalous revelation of, and invitation to, the female body. The one is discovered as a symptom of the other, with death being the only available solution and punishment. By implication, chastity, a virtue that cannot actually be seen, emerges as a quality that must necessarily be performed, in other contexts and through alternative techniques.

Mariam's mistreatment and execution, therefore, can be read, at one level, as ideology in practice: attitudes hostile to women are granted a dramatic articulation. The queen refuses the performance expected of her, and she dies because a false cultural perception about femininity is believed to have a grounding in 'reality'. Eschewing a defence of herself against untenable charges, Mariam is figured as both disobedient wife and unruly subject, since she resists Herod's husbandly and kingly requirements. Yet, confident of her own innocence, Mariam can lay claim to a martyr's death. The queen, along with Constabarus, aims at a martyrological construction on more than one occasion. Matching such interpretive gestures, the messenger describes Mariam's conduct at execution as 'stately . . . not debased by fear; / Her look did seem to keep

15

the world in awe, / Yet mildly did her face this fortune bear' (V, 26–8). The martyrological features of the description take on a heightened significance in that the queen's death, as several critics have noted, partakes of the crucifixion: the butler who betrays Mariam at Salome's behest hangs himself from a tree in a clear evocation of Judas Iscariot, while references to the resurrection help to identify Mariam as a second Christ. Herod's bitter regret after the queen's death, her final silencing and his desperate yearning again to hear her voice might, in this light, be construed as the signs of Mariam's victory, albeit one that can be earned only inside a misogynist context. But the resolution of Mariam's transgression does not exorcize all ambiguity. Margaret W. Ferguson points out that the manner of Mariam's death – a beheading – means that the queen parallels not only Christ at this moment but also Mary, Queen of Scots, and Anne Boleyn.[6] Both of these historical personages, of course, connote an out-of-control sexuality, and both were figures extending beyond the conventional bounds of femininity (Boleyn through witchcraft, and Mary, Queen of Scots, through a treasonable bid for power). Ferguson does not tease out the point, but the analogy at once pushes the play's martyrological elements onto these two executed female unfortunates, establishing them, in an implicit indictment of Henry VIII and Elizabeth I, as victims of monarchical abuse and injustice. The alignment with Mary, Queen of Scots, is particularly suggestive. It draws attention to Mariam's religious alterity as a Jewess, supporting Ferguson's thesis that 'behind the figure of the non-compliant Mariam lies ... a cultural discursive construction that we might label ''minority religious dissent'' '.[7] At the same time, it complicates the clarity of the play's gender/power demarcations. Like Mariam, Mary, Queen of Scots, was betrayed by another woman (Elizabeth I), a relative who, like Salome, was able to cast a smoke-screen over her part in the execution order. This final echo of the circumstances surrounding the death of this sixteenth-century claimant to the English throne reminds us of the extent to which gender, and gendered conflict, play a significant part in the action leading to Mariam's demise.

Crucially, what condemns Mariam is not only a cultural equation between speech and a lack of chastity, but also the manner in which such a formula is linguistically exploited by other women. In this connection, the role of the queen's sister-in-law is vital. Salome's expedient deployment of language (she convinces her brother to execute her enemies, which allows her to pursue a new lover while still wreaking revenge) enables the play to point up an alternative role model for the speaking female. In fact, Salome's presence in *The Tragedy of Mariam* highlights speech as a route to power rather than a guarantor of disenfranchisement. By outwardly performing a compliance to gender norms that Mariam refuses to enact, Salome secures her desires, confounding conventional moral and generic conventions and avoiding the censure of villainy. Diane Purkiss argues that 'this should be read less as an endorsement of Salome than as a reflection of a stoic disdain for the operations of the world upon virtue'.[8] Alternatively, however, one might argue that Salome's ability to evade punishment functions just as intriguingly as a fantasy of female empowerment on Cary's part.

Whereas Mariam's speech is separated from her sexuality (contrary to Herod's convictions, the queen is both loquacious and chaste), Salome's linguistic freedom is dependent, at least in part, upon her exploitation of the possibilities inherent in the 'whore' designation. Any moral scruples about arranging her husband's murder are pushed to one side in Salome's recognition that she has no inherent virtue to uphold; as she comments, ' 'Tis long ago/ Since shame was written on my tainted brow' (I, 282–3). The acknowledgement of an alternative course for her life, and the awareness of the opportunities afforded by a conventional morality ('Had I affected an unspotted life,/ Joseph's veins had still been stuffed with blood/ And I to him had lived a sober wife', I, 286–8), embrace the kind of pragmatics that, elsewhere, Mariam rejects. Salome's active shaping of her own life and relationships stands in stark contrast to Mariam's passive refusal to agitate to help her own cause. Despite her own realization, later echoed by her husband, that she 'could enchain [Herod] with a smile/ And lead him captive with a gentle word' (III, 163–4), Mariam disdains to use her power of speech to clear her own name. At once the play constructs this act as both completely noble ('Mine innocence is hope enough for me', III, 180) and foolishly stubborn (if Mariam had but 'bent', concludes the chorus, she would be 'free from fear, as well as innocent', III, 249–50). The ambiguity of this double-sided elaboration of the character complicates still further the ethics of Mariam's actions in comparison with Salome's more arch machinations. However female agency is enacted in *The Tragedy of Mariam*, it is attacked and arraigned. There would appear to be no easy way whereby women can secure social and intellectual autonomy. No one means of acquiring and maintaining female virtue and integrity is accounted entirely satisfactory.

Mariam's status as heroine is further interrogated by another female character – Doris, Herod's ex-wife. At the climax of her rousing farewell speech, as she declares that she is unafraid to die because her 'soul is free from adversary's power' (IV, 569), Mariam is confronted, in a moment charged with theatrical tension, by Doris, her greatest opponent. Doris endeavours to undo the notion of Mariam's self-satisfied purity through an accusation of adultery. Because Herod's divorce was unlawful, Doris argues, Mariam has been living in sin. The queen's aspirations to a quasi-sanctified condition are also thrown into relief by the eloquent relation of Doris' own suffering (abandonment and the pronouncement that her children are illegitimate) under patriarchal rule. This is a mode of suffering in which Mariam is directly implicated, since her beauty is cited as one reason for Doris' plight; as Herod's ex-wife laments, 'Mariam's purer cheek/ Did rob from mine the glory' (II, 223–4). The subsequent quarrel between the women offsets the tone of Mariam's final speech, and stamps the concluding stages not so much with the hallmarks of a sublime transcendence as of a verbal skirmish. As a result, the messenger's later report of the queen's dignified death is compromised and can only come across as an imperfect account of events.

In her condemnation of Mariam, Doris' description of the queen's skin as 'purer' offers a telling instance of the ways in which beauty in the play is invariably evoked in racialized terms. Dympna Callaghan has recently argued that race is 'actually part of the manifest content' of Cary's Palestinian-set drama.[9] Drawing attention to the racialization of the Jew in early modern England, Callaghan demonstrates that the construction of Herod as a conventional racialized Jew is part and parcel of his discovery as a tyrannical monarch–husband. But racialization is no less essential to the play's elaborations of female rivalry, which are primarily conveyed via tropes of beauty. The women in *The Tragedy of Mariam* are distinguished by, and registered through, a language of physical attractiveness. Beauty is represented as a competition, as a means to secure male admiration and as a subsequent route to power. Doris is displaced by Mariam's superior physical virtues, while Mariam herself is constantly measured against a metaphorical background of famous beauties such as Cleopatra and Livia. The key measure of beauty in the play is the possession of paleness. Like Shakespeare's Desdemona, Mariam is invariably described in terms of fairness, lightness and whiteness, a descriptive process which increases as she moves towards death. Ideal beauty, for Mariam, is firmly rooted in a paler skin and a higher class location. When grieving for her death, Herod suggests that Mariam, by virtue of her racial elevation and socially superior position, is far above a darker-skinned woman; he also associates her beauty with her regal identity:

> Why shine you sun? . . .
> . . . my Mariam's dead!
> You could but shine if some Egyptian blowze,
> Or Ethiopian dowdy lose her life.
> This was . . .
> The King of Jewry's fair and spotless wife!
>
> (V, 193–8)

In contrast to Mariam's physical appearance, Salome's beauty, while recognized by some, is more often denigrated in racialized rhetoric. Herod states that Salome, when placed alongside Mariam, appears 'a sunburnt blackamoor' (IV, 461) and 'an ape' (IV, 459); earlier, her darker complexion is seen as the signature of an inferior class affiliation. As Mariam exclaims:

> My birth thy baser birth so far excelled
> I had to both of you the princess been.
> Thou parti-Jew and parti-Edomite,
> Thou mongrel, issued from rejected race!
>
> (I, 233–6)

19

The speech makes clear that complementary racial and class differences are thought to obtain between different strands of the Jewish lineage (the Edomites and Jacob's descendants), and that Salome must therefore be disallowed from laying claim to a superlative aesthetic register.

By contrast, Salome refuses to brook any form of differentiation. Her retorts to the slurs visited upon her suggest that she subscribes to the notion of a common humanity. 'What odds betwixt your ancestors and mine?/ Both born of Adam ... And both did come from holy Abraham's line' (I, 240–42), she demands, emphasizing the materiality of a shared geneaology. More generally in the play, Salome is privileged as the voice not only of a common humanity but of a gendered collective. Although she behaves in an individualist fashion and puts her own needs first, Salome is also the spokesperson for defences of womankind in a series of wonderfully impassioned speeches. Typical here are comments such as 'Given to [men], why barred from women?' (I, 306) and 'Cannot women hate as well as men?' (I, 308), which posit the vibrancy of a gender alliance that rises above divisive and segregating preoccupations. And, on occasions, such a schema of female solidarity is presented as enabling social emancipation, as when Salome argues that she will 'show my sex the way to freedom's door' (I, 310). In her arguments for gendered union, and in her dismissal of physical categorizations, Salome embodies yet another challenge to the dictates and practices of seventeenth-century ideological institutions.

It is the superimposition of one modality of identification upon another that makes the rivalry between women in *The Tragedy of Mariam* so dramatically arresting, and gender, race and class are the necessary parts of this successful theatrical equation. With the exception of Callaghan's work on race, critics have tended to focus, to the exclusion of all else, on the play's gendered considerations. However, the provision of numerous foils to Mariam and Herod reveals that neither tyranny, nor reactions to it, can be slotted into gender-specific classifications (neither men nor women are figured as occupying one-dimensional positions). In this sense, Cary is unique in furnishing for her audience a dazzling array of thematic concatenations and combinations, reading gender conflict through the lens of race, and understanding race via the mechanism of class contention.

The Tragedy of Mariam is a play which entertains complexity and difficulty as its key concerns. Complexity, after all, is central to Mariam's opening realization. In a densely wrought metaphor that shows her affinity to Caesar, Mariam berates herself for the frequency with which she has attacked the Roman leader 'for deceit/ Because he wept when Pompey's life was gone?/ Yet, when he lived, he thought his name too great' (I, 2–4). These self-recriminations go hand in hand with Mariam's articulation of a mixed reaction to Herod's putative death: 'at his death your eyes true drops did rain,/ Whom dead, you did not wish alive again' (I, 12–13), she observes. The coming together of two emotional responses leads Mariam to acknowledge that entertaining oppositional lines of thought at one and the same time is not impossible, nor even necessarily hypocritical. Her dilemma, I would argue, then, is not simply that of being and seeming (as the critical consensus has maintained); rather, her difficulties are located in contradiction, in simultaneity and in internal irresolution. In this sense, Mariam rests as a sensitive barometer of the fluctuations of the play in the same moment as she stands as a cipher for the situation of seventeenth-century women wrestling with the densities and contrarieties of their lived experience.

2

Poetry

GENRE, RANGE, WRITERS

Poetry written by women in the seventeenth century was disseminated in multiple ways. For seventeenth-century England was a culture in which both print and manuscript were valued as legitimate forms of literary activity, and women's poetry is no exception to the rule. Large numbers of poems by women were printed soon after they were composed, either in editions lacking authorial consent or in collections approved and overseen by the authors. Other writers, both male and female, shunned print culture. The elitist avoidance of a commercial stigma may have been a factor here, since manuscript circulation inhabited a more socially exclusive territory than print; alternatively, for women, the risk of being charged with immodesty was no doubt an inhibiting consideration. Certainly, many seventeenth-century women elected to circulate poetry in manuscript copies, the term 'manuscript' connoting both a single sheet containing a transcription of one poem and more extensive compilations of verse, which would have been copied out by friends, professional scribes or the poets themselves. Poems by women could also be found in ephemeral manifestations, including popular ballads and songs. Less ephemeral but contrasting in form again are such literary exercises as epitaphs, which were written by women for use on funeral monuments. To appreciate the range of poetry written by women, then, it is necessary to determine the relationship between the author and particular modes of production, and to speculate about a full participation by female poets in the literary modalities the period provided.

Inside different systems of circulation, women's poetry met varying fates. While many were passed over or received a hostile reception, the works of other women became generally known and garnered public esteem. The poetry of Katherine Philips, for example, an aristocratic poet writing prolifically in the 1650s and 1660s, was widely reproduced and circulated. That her work was published in one unauthorized edition and at least three authorized editions during the seventeenth century is testimony to her popularity in the social imaginary. To function as a writing woman poet in the period was not necessarily to experience anonymity.

Within the recent recuperation of early modern women's writing, the traditionally valued genre of poetry, along with drama, has tended to attract the most sustained critical attention. Key articles and studies have focused upon individual poets, while substantial amounts of women's poetry have been reprinted or, in the case of manuscript poets, printed for the first time. Although single-author editions continue to be less frequent in number, Germaine Greer's groundbreaking *Kissing the Rod*, first published in 1988, has been followed up by several collections devoted exclusively to seventeenth-century women's poetic output.[1] Abundantly evident, in this connection, is the distance covered since the publication of the Greer anthology. One of the most recent collections, for instance – Jane Stevenson and Peter Davidson's *Early Modern Women Poets*, which, published in 2001, represents the latest research into women's poetry – solves many outstanding questions of attribution, looks beyond lists of printed books to embrace previously unpublished manuscript poems and indicates the extent to which the diversity of seventeenth-century women's poetry is only now being adequately acknowledged.[2]

In their chosen accompaniments, and in the poems they elect to include, the newest anthologies present themselves as useful guides to mapping the nature of the field. From an initial inspection of this work, it is clear that an immediate effect has been to push a number of key figures to the critical forefront. Lengthy selections in *Early Modern Women Poets* from newly canonical figures such as Aemilia Lanyer, Katherine Philips and Aphra Behn indicate the now universally recognized importance of these writers as central poetic personalities.

Besides the sheer volume of their writings, poets such as Lanyer, Philips and Behn have also come to prominence because of their modern resonances. Thus Lanyer's *Salve Deus Rex Judaeorum* (1611), which forms the basis of this chapter's case study, retells the story of the Passion from the viewpoint of the women who spectated upon it.[3] The author's woman-centred perspective, her creation of a community of 'good women' and her endeavour, in a section entitled 'Eve's Apology', to rescue Eve from the Augustan charge that women are to blame for the fall of humanity have won the notice of contemporary critics keen to construct seventeenth-century women writers as 'oppositional voices', as transgressors of normative ideologies.[4]

An emphasis upon the creation of networks between women links Lanyer's work to the second newly canonical figure, Katherine Philips. Poems extracted in *Early Modern Women Poets*, such as 'Friendship's Mysteries: To My Dearest Lucasia', although not answering to the total effect of Philips' output, have attracted comment because of their representation of intimate female relations. Similarly, despite the fact that Behn wrote almost every type of poem imaginable in the last decades of the century, it is her amorous poems such as 'The Disappointment' (telling of Lysander's impotence before Cloris) which tend to stimulate interest, concerned, as they are, with female desire and its ambiguous relation to prevailing gendered ideals of chastity. No doubt because Behn, Lanyer and Philips exploit subject matter of relevance to modern feminist theory, they have become the most prominent names in seventeenth-century poetry, as Margaret J. M. Ezell, in a telling study of the role of ideology in historical recovery, has demonstrated.[5]

If the space devoted to these three writers in *Early Modern Women Poets* is typical of a tendency to reproduce those poets whose agenda and subject matter might most easily be typified as 'feminist', the broader critical trend of which this is a part – that is, the impulse to privilege work which engages directly with the nature of the gendered experience – is also reflected in the collection. Recurring throughout *Early Modern Women Poets* as salient preoccupations are issues of family, marriage, childbirth, child-rearing and, even more urgently, elaborations upon the experience of being a woman writer. Notable in a sizeable proportion of the poems selected is a gendered self-consciousness about the writing process itself. Lanyer's 'Description of Cookham', for example, is self-consciously reflective of the process of producing its own text, simultaneously defending and debasing the poet's decision to enter print and bypassing the responsibility of inspiration in a socially freighted fashion. In the last decades of the seventeenth century, such a gendered consciousness is discovered as assuming an institutional orientation, with poets paying service to traditions of women's writing (hence Behn can explicitly conjure the memory of Philips, using the dead poet both to sanction her work and to establish a sense of an explicitly female writing history). Inviting connections between women writers across the seventeenth century, the anthology, through its selections, underscores the ties that bind female poets and the trajectories into which their work might be inserted.

While the selections in *Early Modern Women Poets* engage with current opinion, privileging poems by key figures which convey either the gendered experience or the experience of being a woman writer, the anthology simultaneously advances in an opposite critical direction. The depth and variety of women's forays into verse are fully attested to here, with a generous selection of religious, political and vernacular poetry featuring alongside more canonical extracts: the inescapable conclusion is that the parameters of the field are considerably wider than those drawn up by an earlier critical generation.

The eclectic mixture presented in *Early Modern Women Poets* points up the fact that many women versified primarily as a religious exercise, although this took different forms according to the status of the writer and her particular social location. Inside the broad spectrum of Protestantism, one encounters women writers of various classes writing in multiple ways and producing poetry that fell into no one simple typological category. Often poems are contained in books which combine passages of verse with prosaic reflections. The poems of Anne Greenwell, a Quaker preacher writing in the 1650s and beyond, for example, are extracted from her spiritual diary and register the introverted, analytical and changeable tone which characterized the daily tussle

of self-examination. The more mainstream religious meditations of Jane Cheyne, the daughter of William Cavendish, Duke
of Newcastle, which are largely composed of prayers and
biblical interpretation (they date from the 1640s onwards),
reinforce the private inflection of much poetry of a religious
nature. Such are the material circumstances within which the
poems function, to the extent that the poetry of both Greenwell
and Cheyne highlights the necessity of recognizing the context
informing the poem and adjusting reading assumptions accordingly. However, the simultaneously didactic quality of some
poetry (work may have circulated within a *coterie* of friends and
relatives or even, in the case of Cheyne, been appended to a
funeral oration) forcefully suggests the public utility of verse as
an example or lesson to others. The line between individual
versifying and the wider world is further blurred when one
bears in mind the subsequent uses to which ostensibly private
verse could be put. Even before the outbreak of the Civil War,
many private exercises were deployed as propaganda. Having
circulated privately in manuscript for some years, for instance,
Alice Sutcliffe's *Meditations of Man's Mortality* was published in
1633 and again in 1634 on behalf of the Puritan cause as an
implicit arraignment of excesses at the court of Charles I.
Despite the initial impetus of much women's verse, then, the
public arena might have been as powerful a sphere of operation
as the private domain: no poem could be straitjacketed in terms
of its actual and potential circulation and applicability.

Matching the numbers of women who wrote ostensibly for
personal use are those female poets who composed poetry out
of an explicit engagement with contemporary political events:
the Great Fire of London, the 'Popish Plot', the Restoration of
the Monarchy and the Glorious Revolution are all addressed
directly in seventeenth-century women's verse. The importance of writing as an act of cultural engagement and commentary was particularly pronounced during the Civil War years.
Anne Bradstreet, who emigrated from Northumberland to
America in 1630, published in 1650 *The Tenth Muse*, a volume
which dissects the origins and early years of the Civil War,
expertly situating contemporary politics inside broader historical movements, while Hester Pulter, a committed monarchist,
poignantly protested against the king's arrest in 1647 and went

on to detail related Royalist misfortunes. The polarities span-ned here suggest eloquently that, in women's hands, the genre of poetry can perform more than one ideological task. A case in point is the political pamphlet. In the latter half of the century, such pamphlets, which were produced by radical sectarian women, often added verse interludes or excursions, sometimes in excitingly innovative forms: the Fifth Monarchist, Anna Trapnel, included lengthy poetic interludes in almost all of her prophetic texts, and she is joined by the Baptist, Anne Wentworth, who featured a 'Song of Triumph' in her 1677 defensive tract, *The Vindication of Anne Wentworth*. This sug-gests that, on occasion, a manipulation or blurring of the two modalities of the prose pamphlet and the poetic utterance could be explicitly and consciously mobilized. The role of poetry, in these illustrations, is not circumscribed, and the genre is such that it can be massaged by women to suit any kind of broad social statement.

Nowhere is the consistent flexibility of the poetic form better demonstrated than in the individual case of An Collins. In 1653, the year that Cromwell became Lord Protector of England, Collins published *Divine Songs and Meditations*, a lengthy spiritual autobiography in verse form which deals trenchantly with Civil War politics and attacks, in particular, although not exclusively, the more radical elements involved in the struggle. The markedly autobiographical tenor of the text is indicative of the ways in which the personal and the political cannot be neatly separated out in poetry of the period. This can also be seen both in the work of Bradstreet, who smuggles in political comment via reflection on a particularly gendered migratory experience and writes a long poem about a fire which destroyed the family home, and in the meditations of Pulter, who, when not reflecting upon the treatment accorded the monarch, writes movingly about the death of a young daughter. In these cases, an engagement with national politics feeds into, and is entangled with, the representation of personal trauma. Implicating themselves in the political, these female poets share a kinship with the large numbers of other seventeenth-century women who frame their verse inside elegies to husbands and children and within life-cycles of marriage, childbirth and widowhood.

27

As well as making available a range of women's poems and subject matter, *Early Modern Women Poets* progresses even further down the 'representative' line by including vernacular and ephemeral verse, 'writing which illustrates the way in which verse was used in the relatively oral culture of early modern England for purposes which are not primarily literary, such as libels, slanders, news, instruction, and charms'.[6] Verses in vernacular form may be crafted inexpertly, but they are of considerable interest as historical signs of a vast quotidian circulation of poetry that is now largely untraceable. Moreover, such writing may offer evidence of women's involvement in popular culture, music and same-sex alliances. A song such as 'The Lyke Wake Dirge' (in circulation before 1624), sung at northern English funerals, offers vigorous testimony of women's roles in traditional rural culture. A folk rendition of the Catholic concept of purgatory, it reminds us of the continued activity of female Catholic voices, as does the verse of Gertrude More, a dispossessed Catholic nun writing in the 1630s. With the exception, perhaps, of autobiography, poetry as a genre is vitally important as a medium for communicating a range of voices, those which survive in echoes and refrains and those which persist in more complete and immediate poetic articulations. And acknowledging that women's voices function according to a spectrum of possible types and practices is crucial, for it allows awareness of depth, density, contradiction and discontinuity in an area of writing that might, at first sight, be considered either one-dimensional or predictable.

CASE STUDY: AEMILIA LANYER, *SALVE DEUS REX JUDAEORUM* (1611)

This chapter's case study addresses a precise example of the ways in which seventeenth-century women's poetry operates culturally and ideologically. It focuses on female poets' varied engagements with the patristic tradition concerning original sin, a tradition which becomes particularly prominent in the early seventeenth century but which stretches back to Augustine and indeed St Paul in source.

In *Salve Deus Rex Judaeorum*, Aemilia Lanyer's opening dedication to the queen directly broaches the issue of citation, for it asks Elizabeth if 'Eve's Apology' (the middle section of the poem which utilizes careful biblical exegesis to reduce Eve's culpability for the Fall) 'agrees not with the text' (l. 76) The 'text' that Lanyer refers to is the account of the Fall given in Genesis 3–4 as set out in the Geneva Bible (1594), the key vernacular translation of the Bible preceding the publication of the King James edition in 1611. Lanyer invites Elizabeth, then, to consider the authorial interpretation as one that accords with the biblical source. Beyond its immediately intertextual associations, the question is dangerously generative, since it allows another to be posed, one centred upon the widespread contemporary citation of Genesis: 'And if it do', Lanyer continues, alluding to the 'text', 'why are poor women blamed/ [And] by more faulty men so much defamed?' (ll. 77–8). Here the author makes a forceful connection between contemporary discourses that cite original sin and attitudes towards women overwhelmingly misogynist in nature.

Mary Nyquist points out that it was during the Renaissance that Eve was first positioned as 'a responsible, theologically informed speaking subject': this was a construction of woman which, while offering the possibility of an acknowledgement of her access to knowledge, had the potential to increase Eve's responsibility for the act of original sin.[7] Certainly, contemporary writers such as Joseph Swetnam, who was involved in the *querelle des femmes*, a pamphlet war devoted to castigating women for their supposed faults and misdemeanours, employed Eve in a ruthlessly defamatory fashion. Nor do the ramifications of such a deployment of Eve end only with the verbal. In a discussion of myth and language, Roland Barthes observes that there is invariably a link between myth and its subsequent ideological uses.[8] Lanyer goes on to suggest that the onus of responsibility placed upon Eve for the Fall entails severe social and cultural consequences for women in general.

Many seventeenth-century texts demonstrate the ease with which ideology can move from blaming Eve to legitimizing female oppression. *The Law's Resolution of Women's Rights* (1632) by T. E. recognizes the manoeuvre, noting:

Eve because she had helped to seduce her husband hath inflicted on her an especial bane. *In sorrow shalt thou bring forth thy children, thy desires shall be subject to thy husband, and he shall rule over thee.* See here the reason . . . that women have no voice in parliament . . . and their desires are subject to their husband.[9]

As T. E. makes clear, Eve's divinely ordained punishment (the biblical edict that she should labour painfully in childbirth and be subordinate to her husband) for her originating role in the fall of humanity was, in the sixteenth and seventeenth centuries, a dictating factor in deciding woman's place in contemporary society. Typical of seventeenth-century commentators, T. E. regards Eve's responsibility for the Fall as both an explanation of, and a justification for, woman's inferior status. The interpretation of the Eve narrative is vital, therefore, for it represents one of the great myths through which patriarchy is able to institute its social operations, and such points of contact are germane to Lanyer's elaboration. In particular, what Lanyer identifies as the burden of Eve's conduct is not so much the Fall itself as 'the fault' that is laid 'on patience back,/ That we (poor women) must endure it all' (ll. 793–4). In short, by plotting a route that begins with the single mythic figure of Eve and ends with the collective female gender, Lanyer suggests a heritage for a pejorative construction of women in the popular imagination.

Criticism on Lanyer has tended to take note of the various elements of the poem (such as the representation of a female community and the emphasis upon women's intimate connections with Christ) but to neglect the detailed interplay between these concerns and the central conceit of Adam and Eve. Although 'Eve's Apology' accounts for only 100 lines out of the 2,000 which make up *Salve Deus Rex Judaeorum* as a whole, this section, I argue, because all of the poem's preoccupations refer back to it, is Lanyer's centre-piece. This case study, while concentrating on *Salve Deus Rex Judaeorum*, also briefly explores other renditions of the Fall by two less well-known women poets. Alice Sutcliffe's 'Of Our Loss by Adam' was published in the enlarged 1634 edition of her *Meditations of Man's Mortality*, while Anne Bradstreet included a discussion of Eve in her 1650 poem, 'The Four Ages of Man'. By situating Lanyer inside these related reflections, a specific case for seventeenth-century women's poetic positionings, and antithetically opposed scriptural interpretations, can be made.

'Eve's Apology' is framed by the New Testament story of Pilate's wife. The gulf of communication which obtains between Pilate and his wife – she 'beg[s] her saviour's life', while he refuses to 'hear [her] words' (ll. 751–2) – matches the gender schism manifested throughout the poem. It both anticipates the attempt in the 'Apology' clearly to distinguish between Adam and Eve and parallels Lanyer's construction of Eve and Adam's respective culpability. The 'Apology' begins by emphasizing Eve's essential innocence and the cunning with which the serpent tempts her to sin. States Lanyer:

> Our mother Eve, who tasted of the tree
> . . . .
> Was simply good, and had no power to see;
> The after-coming harm . . .
> The subtle serpent that our sex betrayed,
> Before our fall so sure a plot had laid.
>
> (ll. 763, 765–8)

Recalling St Augustine's assertion that Eve was the weaker and hence more easily deceived of the human alliance, this interpretation eschews the Geneva Bible's notion that Eve sinned with her eyes open and in full cognizance of the implications of her actions. Instead, Lanyer discovers an essential Eve, who is morally innocent, guileless and impressionable. Such an Eve contrasts radically with the figure delineated by Swetnam and departs, too, from the Eve presented in Sutcliffe's *Meditations*. Here, the author's explanations for Eve's behaviour support the traditional idea of her as sensually materialistic: Sutcliffe describes Eve's inability to refuse the fruit as 'incontinent' (*KR* 92), a term often deployed in the period to connote the loss of sexual control resulting from the initial sinful transgression.

Meditations is particularly marked by its emphasis upon Eve's desire to 'excel'. ''Twas pride, made Eve desire still to excel', states Sutcliffe, 'When Satan said, as gods, you then shall be' (*KR* 92). By contrast, Lanyer stresses Eve's thirst for knowledge. Crucially, although Lanyer presents an innocent Eve who is unaware of the consequences of obeying the serpent and taking the fruit, the author is able simultaneously to construct the figure as sufficiently intelligent purposefully to seek out a new knowledge source. 'If Eve did err, it was for knowledge sake' (l. 797), Lanyer states. Biblical exegesis provides one basis for Lanyer's elaboration of knowledge and learning as intimately connected to women and, beyond them, to Eve's actions. To complement this portrayal, Lanyer stresses Adam's apparent ignorance of the function of the fruit, simultaneously contrasting the serpent's persuasiveness with Adam's immediate and unquestioning acceptance. Taking advantage of Genesis' silence on the point, Lanyer suggests that Adam is persuaded merely by the fruit's aesthetic superficiality. She writes: 'The fruit being fair persuaded him to fall; / No subtle serpent's falsehood did betray him' (ll. 797–8). Like Lanyer, Sutcliffe also emphasizes the fact that Adam is not persuaded by the serpent; however, in her poem, the serpent's lure is replaced by the idea that Eve herself deceives her husband into taking the forbidden apple: 'His wife from that obedience soon him drew' (*KR* 91). Animal and human dichotomies are implicitly aligned as Eve assumes the serpent's role, reinforcing through sexual contradistinction the poem's gender divide. An alternative perspective is taken up by Lanyer on this issue, for she is able both to exclude Adam from any claim to the benefits of Eve's acquisition of knowledge and to point up the resultant paradox. 'Yet men will boast of knowledge, which he took / From Eve's fair hand, as from a learned book' (ll. 807–8), Lanyer explains. For Lanyer, then, women are the source of knowledge and wisdom which are stolen and claimed by men who argue that these belong to a masculine preserve.

Continuing to establish Adam's greater responsibility, Lanyer suggests that Adam's authority over Eve means that the culpability for the Fall must rest with him alone. For Eve, according to the poem's logic, cannot be subordinate to Adam and autonomous in the Fall at one and the same time:

> Her fault though great, yet he was most to blame;
> What weakness offered, strength might have refused,
> Being lord of all, the greater was his shame
> . . . .
> For he was lord and king of all the earth.
>
> (ll. 778–80, 783)

A comparable underscoring of Adam's primary responsibility is noticeable in those parts of the poem dedicated to Eve's creation. Although Lanyer concedes that Eve's creation derives from Adam's rib, she goes on to manipulate the myth and to implicate Adam: 'Being made of him, he was the ground of all' (l. 810), the poem declares. Here, as elsewhere in *Salve Deus Rex Judaeorum*, Lanyer resists an easy identification with a contemporary mindset approving of traditional female fallibility.

A simultaneous focus on motherhood in the poem, however, implicitly privileges a female generative power that the creation myth would ostensibly attempt to efface. By explicitly connecting Eve with childbirth from the outset, Lanyer subtly interrogates the plausibility of the figure's derivative origins. At the same time, identifying Eve as mother of all living things subsumes the totality of men and women to a primary idea of motherhood and vaginal birth. The divine punishment of childbirth that was dwelled upon so fervently by contemporary commentators is entirely absent in Lanyer's own imaginative vision. Clearly, the author fails to regard childbirth as a particularly onerous punishment. In contrast, Sutcliffe and Bradstreet's poems associate birth with bodily disease and pain, with 'sorrow, sickness, death and woe' (*KR* 122), and with infection, blood, nausea and female fragility. Moreover, Sutcliffe's consequential attitude to procreation sees the mother as tainted by original sin – 'For as thou now conceive thy seed in sin, / So in great sorrow thou must bring it forth' (*KR* 91) – in a formulation that is strikingly similar to Bradstreet's view that reproduction is sin's eternal and inevitable inheritance: 'Ah me', she states, 'conceived in sin, and born in sorrow' (*KR* 121). Yet for Lanyer women's generative force is reconstructed as a source of power rather than a form of punishment and belittlement. Motherhood is utilized metaphorically to oppose misogyny, with Lanyer stressing men's dependency on a woman being procreative. In the preface 'To the Virtuous Reader', Lanyer criticizes misogynist discourse as the product of 'evil-disposed men, who forgetting they were born of women, nourished of women ... do like vipers deface the wombs wherein they were bred' (ll. 18–20, 22–3). More forcefully, the 'Apology' views childbirth as a reason for men not to oppress women: 'You came not in the world without our pain, / Make that a bar against your cruelty' (ll. 827–8). Arguing against prevailing notions, Lanyer makes a passionate plea for a reformulation of attitudes and a reassessment of women's biological capabilities.

The idea that birth removes women from sin is centred, in *Salve Deus Rex Judaeorum*, upon the iconic figure of the Virgin Mary. Paralleling the discrete delineation of Lanyer's representation of Adam and Eve is the Virgin's absolute demarcation in gender terms: she is one who is 'from all men free' (l. 1078). Lanyer's critical point is that 'it pleased our Lord and Saviour Jesus Christ . . . to be begotten of a woman, born of a woman, nourished of a woman, obedient to a woman' (ll. 39–40, 42–4). The repetition of 'woman' helps to emphasize the importance of woman's position in giving life to God's son, and this is in contrast to the secondary position of man, who is figured as irrelevant to the birth of Christ. Mary, the mother of Jesus, the poem asserts, has now 'freed us from the curse' (l. 1088). By referring to the 'curse' of the Fall, Lanyer stresses the interconnection of the Virgin Mary and Eve. But she also suggests that the act of giving birth to the second Adam, Christ, redeems the place of women in the Christian narrative and establishes an alternative model for the reproductive female. Pursuing this suggestion, Lanyer reworks the arguments of the early church fathers, who represented the Virgin Mary as the second Eve and Christ as the second Adam.[10] The subtitle of Sutcliffe's work ('Of Our Loss by Adam, and Our Gain by Christ; the First Adam was Made a Living Soul, the Second Adam a Quickening Spirit; for as in Adam We All Die, So in Christ, shall All be Made Alive', *KR* 91) suggests a comparable intervention. The poem refers to the parallel which is often made between Adam, who was responsible for the Fall, and Christ, who represented the subsequent route to salvation. A similar analogy can be found in Lanyer's poem when she juxtaposes the loss through 'Adam's fall' (l. 259) with the salvation of mankind, 'raised by a Judas-kiss' (l. 260).

Despite its highlighted presence on her title page, Sutcliffe sees no emancipatory potential in conventional theology. Indeed, with reference to the punishments described in the Bible, she states: 'Obedience to thy husband yield thou must' (*KR* 91). More arresting in this respect is Lanyer, who finds in the theological wisdoms of her time the basis of an entirely new heterosexual arrangement. The poem's dedication to Lady Katherine, Countess of Suffolk, for example, implies that Christ supersedes Adam in relation to Eve's female descendants: 'Here they may see a lover much more true / Than ever was since first the world began' (ll. 52–3), the author avers. The idea that Christ prompts a rethinking of the power dynamic of the heterosexual relationship is reflected in his description. Critics have noticed that Lanyer's Christ is feminine both in appearance and character. He has the passive qualities traditionally associated with women, such as humility, grace, mildness, obedience, meekness, patience and silence, while his physical description is of a man who:

> appears so fair,
> So sweet, so lovely in his spouse's sight,
> That unto snow we may his face compare,
> His cheeks like scarlet, and his eyes so bright
> . . . .
> His head is likened to the finest gold,
> His curled locks so beauteous to behold.
>
> (ll. 1305–8, 1311–12)

What has not received notice is the extent to which this description of Christ also conforms to contemporary traditions of describing the romance hero, a representational process seen to its best advantage in Sir Philip Sidney's *Arcadia*, which was first published in 1590. Christ, then, may be a feminized point of identification in *Salve Deus Rex Judaeorum*, but he is also an object of eroticism for Lanyer's readers and tantalizes with a gender-free model of heterosexual possibilities. The idealized relationship sketched out between women and Christ – Christ is represented as the 'lover' and 'bridegroom' to pious women – replaces Adam, the husband, in the Edenic story. By implication, disappearing as well are those elements of female subordination that contemporary readers looked for in Genesis and found ratified by that source.

In the closing stanzas of 'Eve's Apology', the semantic 'fall' (l. 759), then, has a double meaning, since it refers both to Eve's transgression and to the crucifixion of Christ in the New Testament. By summoning the New Testament,

Lanyer represents men's actions as liberating Eve from her culpability; the woman's fault, it is implied, is insignificant in comparison to the male persecution of Christ: 'Till now your indiscretion sets us free, / And makes our former fault much less appear' (ll. 761–2). Lanyer's careful demarcation of the Passion along gender lines – the author draws attention to the differing attitudes of men and women to the crucifixion, paralleling the two sexes throughout – leads carefully up to this point and to this climactic announcement. Interestingly, by gendering the Passion narrative, Lanyer is permitted to reinvent the mythic creation of Adam in much the same way that writers involved in the *querelle des femmes* negatively interpreted Eve's derivative creation. Genesis 2:7 describes how 'The Lord God also made the man of the dust of the ground, and breathed in his face breath of life, and the man was a living soul', and it is to this verse that Lanyer alludes when she describes the male apostles who abandon Christ as 'scorpions bred in Adam's mud' (l. 381). Likewise, those who orchestrated Christ's crucifixion, it is claimed, originated in 'wretched worldlings made of dust and earth' (l. 675). Both representations depend upon an idea of reproduction that excludes female generative power and locates the source of sin in Adam's parthenogenetic creativity.

By attempting to exonerate Eve (or, at least, to lessen her culpability) through the use of a comparative method of typology, Lanyer engineers a more egalitarian representational dispensation, lessening the significance of the Edenic story and emphasizing the New Testament as its successor. The parallel between these two major biblical components is essential to an understanding of Lanyer's assertive use of the past tense in one of the poem's climactic sequences. 'Let not us women glory in men's fall / Who had power given to over-rule us all' (ll. 759–60), Lanyer states, suggesting that the divine command which authorized the subordination of woman to man has been displaced (or even effaced) by exclusively male processes of Christian persecution. Espousing this perspective, Lanyer creates a position from which she is able to attack the use of the myth as a justification for contemporary sexual inequality. 'Your fault being greater, why should you disdain / Our being your equals, free from tyranny?' (ll. 829–30), the poem de-

mands. The language of liberation deployed here, one sus-
pects, reflects autobiographically back upon Lanyer and upon
the restrictions and burdens placed upon her subjectivity by
Eve's mythic transgressions; by the same token, a rhetoric of
political absolutism highlights that related preoccupation of
Salve Deus Rex Judaeorum, which is the oppression of women
by their masculine counterparts.

In a recent study of myth and literature, William Righter
draws attention to the political and radical aspects of mythic
deconstruction. The 'freedom from myth', he observes, 'is a
preface to action'.[11] The Edenic myth is not an immutable
entity, and, although she begins the 'Apology' by ratifying
Eve's weak and derivative status, Lanyer is able to end with a
radical plea to her contemporary society for sexual equality.
The brief discussions of Sutcliffe and Bradstreet which have
also formed part of this chapter may suggest that such a poetic
positioning is not specifically related to gender. These positions notwithstanding, it is certainly the case that Lanyer's
follow-up plea – 'let us have our liberty again' (l. 825) –
signifies nothing less than a desire to return to a pre-Fall stage
where both sexes stood on an equal footing. Attempting a
reconciliation between, on the one hand, a society in which
women were subordinated and, on the other, a mythic Eden in
which men and women may have enjoyed equivalence, Lanyer
demonstrates the radical potential of poetically negotiating
Genesis, the foundational biblical narrative.

3

Mothers' Advice Books

GENRE, RANGE, WRITERS

In seventeenth-century terms, the mothers' legacies of Elizabeth Joscelin and Dorothy Leigh were 'bestsellers'. *The Mother's Legacy to Her Unborn Child* by Joscelin, which forms the case study for this chapter, ran through eight editions between 1624 and 1684, while Leigh's *The Mother's Blessing* amassed twenty-three editions between 1616 and 1674, making it by far the most frequently printed text by a female author in the period.[1] Mothers' advice books occupy a singular place among the other works addressed in this study because their various reprintings mean that this genre of writing spanned the century. To contemporary eyes, the legacies of Joscelin and Leigh appear to have contained broad relevancies that crossed the decades and appealed to a range of historical consumers.

In essence, this type of advice book is founded upon the mother leaving counsel, in the form of a written legacy or benediction, that will speak for her after death. Thomas Goad, the editor of the 1632 printing of *The Mother's Legacy to Her Unborn Child*, describes a work that will stand as 'a deputed mother for instruction'; in a similar vein, Leigh, speaking for herself, is hopeful in her volume that 'this my mind will continue long after me in writing' (*WW* 23).[2] Mothers' advice books, then, are designed to function *in loco parentis*; they substitute for the moral and religious teaching of the maternal figure, completing the task of nurturing the child to maturity. As befits such a weighty responsibility, the mother's advice book rehearses a multiplicity of themes and subjects. Hence, Leigh's *The Mother's Blessing* devotes itself to such far-reaching matters as how to choose a name for a child, which books to reserve for leisure reading, and the means whereby wives and servants can be selected. Such literary and domestic discussions notwithstanding, the mother's advice book is more generally slanted towards answering questions about the maintenance of a Christian life: all of the works belonging to this genre offer spiritual guidance and orientation in religious practice and education.

Because the mother's advice book is constructed as a private, intimate exchange between mother and child, the authors explicitly conjure their children as the intended audience. 'To my children . . . the readers of this book' (*WW* 18) writes Leigh, and she is joined by Joscelin, who directs herself 'not to the world but to mine own child' (*WW* 111). A reader, therefore, at an immediate level, is placed in the position of voyeur: he or she is the unexpected spectator who has stumbled upon a personal and exclusive moment between parent and offspring. Despite such an ostensible bias, the deployment of particular preoccupations and the frequent utilization of a didactic tone attest to a readership that stretches beyond the merely familial. For, outside Joscelin's assertions that she writes for her own child, the recognition that her work may 'come to the world's eye' (*WW* 111) freely circulates. Likewise, the wording on the title page of Leigh's *The Mother's Blessing* is ambiguously phrased: her 'blessing' is simultaneously 'left behind for her children' and, boasting 'many good exhortations and godly admonitions', composed 'for all parents' (*WW* 15).

As her title page suggests, Leigh's work is cognizant of attracting a larger readership; in fact, although mothers' advice books posit a younger consumer, they actually inform an adult audience. Nor, despite Leigh's frequent use of the 'we women' formulation, is the audience necessarily imagined as female. Rather, these texts appear to be aimed at men as potential users. Leaving to one side her overall tone of deference to the patriarch, Joscelin firmly and precisely tutors her husband in how to manage the child's upbringing. Similarly, the advice in Leigh's volume about selecting a wife and running a household is only suitable for adult sons. Moreover, both books constantly shade into general discussions, suggesting that they are pitched at sons and husbands beyond an immediately familial environment. Presumably, the intended buyer – the purchaser who was in part responsible for sending mothers' advice books to the top of the 'bestseller' list – was masculine. Here, then, is an intriguing possibility: in the success of mothers' advice books, we can glimpse an instance of a woman's voice providing authoritative counsel (which was openly accepted) to male listeners and readers in the public domain.

While Leigh and Joscelin's mothers' advice books proved among the first examples of the genre, earlier instances can still be located. Pertinent in this connection is Nicholas Breton's impersonation of a female, maternal voice in *The Mother's Blessing* (1602); relevant, too, is the Catholic Elizabeth Grymeston's collection of meditations, prayers and advice, *Miscellanea. Meditations. Memoratives*, which was written for the guidance of her son and published in 1604.[3] All of these texts are both a product of, and an aid to, meditating on death, an urgent and popular contemporary enterprise. Crucially, Leigh writes not simply in anticipation of her legacy after death; rather, she composes from a *near*-death position, with her work being constructed as a dying mother's last testament. The title page of her *The Mother's Blessing* styles the work 'the godly counsel of a gentlewoman not long since deceased' (*WW* 15), and, throughout the narrative, the author highlights herself as one 'going out of the world' (*WW* 17) who 'cannot long be here to speak unto you' (*WW* 23). Grymeston's volume is no less suffused with the prospect of an imminent demise. Her posthumous narrative situates her as a mother about to 'yield to this languishing consumption . . . a dead woman among the living' (Grymeston, A3ʳ). In privileging perspectives stimulated by a mortal proximity, these mothers' advice books avail themselves of the authority proverbially implicit in expiring pronouncements. Indeed, it might be argued that the freedom with which the mothers' advice book writers speak is directly related to the verbal emancipation permitted by the death-bed experience.

Mothers' advice books can be contextualized no less usefully in terms of the promotion, by sixteenth-century Protestant reformers, of household godliness – in particular, the mother's duty to instruct male and female children in spiritual matters. *The Mother's Legacy to Her Unborn Child* sets against each other a father's desire to provide a child with a material legacy and a maternal need to secure a spiritual inheritance: 'men purchase land and store up treasure for their unborn babes . . . I am careful for thy salvation being such an eternal portion' (*WW* 110–11), Joscelin states. In many ways, mothers' advice books merely appropriate and translate into a written format the responsibility women were generally seen to have for instructing children. Typical of the authors under consideration in this chapter, Leigh writes so that her sons will receive the religious teaching that she, as a mother, is duty-bound to provide. The writer additionally discovers her work not just as a maternal duty but also as a wifely requirement, an act undertaken to obey her late husband who urged her, on the point of expiry, to ensure that his sons were 'well instructed' (*WW* 17). Mothers' advice books, then, are developed as an extension to the legitimate domestic roles of mother and wife, as these identities were elaborated in seventeenth-century cultural practice.

In keeping with such a emphasis upon household duties and expectations, the writers are keen to stress a forceful maternal bond as one justification for authorship. The original impetus for writing, it is argued, emanates from a sense of motherly zeal. Notable here is Grymeston, who sees the strength of her maternal devotion, and the impulse to the authorial act, as inextricably related; as she states, 'there is no love so forcible as the love of an affectionate mother to her natural child . . . no mother can . . . more naturally manifest her affection than in advising her children' (Grymeston, A3^r). The bringing together in this passage of motherly affection and general advice is presented as a perfectly acceptable manoeuvre, one that, because rooted in the 'natural' order, has a godly sanction. Adopting a comparable rhetoric, Leigh asks that 'no man blame a mother, though she something exceed in writing to her children, since every man knows that the love of a mother to her children is hardly contained within the bounds of reason' (*WW* 23). Excesses of writing are tied to, and precipitated by, excesses of maternity, and both are seen to have been shaped by biological determinants.

If mothers' advice books can be contextualized in terms of popular reflections, they can be located no less powerfully in

41

terms of themselves. Several contemporary references demonstrate that both Leigh and Joscelin's volumes were well known, suggesting that, together, the authors produced work which set influential standards. Their shared 'legacy' was a model to experiment with and imitate. It may not be surprising, then, that the mother's advice genre continued to prosper in female hands well into the eighteenth century. Certainly, it is possible to see later books of maternal advice as stimulated by Leigh and Joscelin's example. Elizabeth Clinton's *The Countess of Lincoln's Nursery* (1622) is addressed to her daughter-in-law. In trenchant prose, it rehearses Leigh's godly mother's preference for breast-feeding to argue that women should breast-feed their own children rather than, as was often the case, employing wet-nurses. Also indebted is M. R.'s *The Mother's Counsel or Live Within Compass*, which was published *c.* 1630 and addressed to a daughter, albeit a younger one. It aspires, with Leigh's advice book, to the status of a last will and testament. No less reflective of its predecessors is Elizabeth Richardson's *A Lady's Legacy to Her Daughters* (1645); although written in the form of prayers for specific occasions and circumstances, the text clearly borrows from Joscelin and Leigh not only in terms of its title but also in terms of its generic affiliations. Later seventeenth-century examples confirming Leigh and Joscelin's continuing vitality include Susanna Bell's *The Legacy of a Dying Mother to Her Mourning Children* (1673), an oral narrative transcribed by a neighbour attending on the author in her final hours, Anne Wentworth's 1677 poem, 'A Mother's Legacy to Her Daughter', and the anonymous *The Mother's Blessing: Being Several Godly Admonitions Given by a Mother unto Her Children upon Her Death-Bed*, which was published in 1685. These are only among the most popular texts belonging to the genre: other instances abound. Moreover, sizeable quantities of mothers' advice, such as Lady Anne Halkett's poems, 'Mother's Will to Her Unborn Child' (1656) and 'To My Son, Robert Halkett' (1670), remain in manuscript.[4] Even in other literary genres, the dictating role of the mother's advice book can be detected. Advisory women's poems have already been alluded to, but there were also female dedications that partook of maternal counsel and autobiographies immersed in motherly admonitions. For instance, the autobiographies, scriptural meditations and medical papers of Lady Grace Mildmay, a Tudor gentlewoman, feature addresses to her daughter and instructions about the upbringing and education of the author's grandchildren.[5] The extent of such examples leads to the suspicion that the concerns of Leigh and Joscelin were symptomatic of larger female interests in the period, and that the writers' work exerted a significant pressure on women's interventions in other literary genres.

The formative role of mothers' advice books suggests that, during the seventeenth century, it was perfectly possible for women to construct a legitimate and authoritative speaking voice, albeit one centred upon a mother in her final hours. In a recent article, Kristen Poole has comprehensively established the complementary range of strategies deployed in the mother's advice narrative, highlighting the genre's careful application of biblical justifications and contemporary discourses of maternity and mortality.[6] Yet over and above the volumes' self-conscious manipulations and purposeful invocations of recognizable frames of reference, an anxiety about authorial unsuitability and a potentially negative reception still remained. One might argue, in fact, that, despite textual triumphs in the genre, broader assumptions about women and writing rested unaffected. Comments recorded by the mothers' advice book writers themselves are illuminating here. Acknowledging writing as 'a thing so unusual among us [women]' (WW 22), Leigh anticipates 'censure' (WW 18), while Richardson views her industry as an 'endeavour . . . contemptible to many because a woman's' (WW 164). In a complementary fashion, all the authors assume an adversely critical stance in relation to the quality of their writerly productions. 'Unworthy' is the adjective enlisted by Richardson to typify her 'poor labour' (WW 162); Leigh likens the publication of her book to a demonstration of her 'imperfections to . . . the world' (WW 18). Behind such pejorative constructions of their own activities lies an implicit endorsement by the mothers' advice book writers of traditional feminine shortcomings and incapacities. 'I thought of writing', states Joscelin, for example, 'but then mine own weakness appeared so manifestly that I was ashamed and durst not undertake it' (WW 106). The speaking voice agitating within the genre, therefore, was apparently at odds with tendencies pulling in the opposite direction, even if the constructions of female virtue delineated belonged with established ideological stereotypes. The result was a series of works that, in their registration of reticence and inadequacy, belied the visibility of the form and the volume of maternal counsel generated.

But the elaboration of reservations (which, in and of themselves, constituted a paradoxical condition of publication) in mothers' advice books did not prevent an engagement with urgent contemporary questions. Because mothers' advice books reflect upon the observation of a Christian life, they confront and negotiate a central seventeenth-century equation between household piety and the spiritual health of the nation. Given pervasive analogies circulating in the early modern period between the microcosmic family and the macrocosmic state, the significance of maternal counsel's broader cogitations should not be underestimated. Mothers' advice books also extend beyond these parameters. Both Leigh and Joscelin explore the advantages and disadvantages of spontaneous and timetabled prayer, Sunday observances, the uses of wealth and the persistence of Catholic doctrine in the Protestant liturgy, matters which, at the time, belonged with a vital public discussion of the Reformation's social effects. In particular, Joscelin and Leigh utilize their desire that their sons be ministers as an excuse simultaneously to ratify, and criticize, the preaching discipline; most obviously, they catalogue examples of preachers and preaching styles which should and should not be imitated. To enter print for the mothers' advice book writers, then, was not to restrict an empowering use of the authorial space, once that had been created.

Moreover, while mothers' advice books defer to masculine authority at a general level, they simultaneously entertain a potentially dissident perspective. At several points, Leigh, in particular, wanders away from her ostensible subject to mount defences of womankind. In articulating adamantine views about the responsibilities due to the wife (who should be treated as a 'companion and fellow . . . [since] she is always too good to be thy servant and worthy to be thy fellow', WW 32), the author offers an implicit challenge to a domestic system that might consign the female spouse to abusive drudgery.

More broadly, because her commentary is founded upon biblical narratives, Leigh's remarks work to deflate misogynist notions circulating in contemporary culture. Passages animated by the figure of Susanna are put to work positively to highlight the female virtue of chastity (in contrast to conventionally male constructions of seduction and rape), while discussions based upon the examples of Eve and Mary throw into stark relief prevalent myths about the gendered complexion of sin, transgression, reproduction and language.

As the case study makes clear, mothers' advice books are both didactic and deferring, 'safe' and confrontational: they are situated at one and the same time within the household and the public arena. In fact, the discontinuities inherent in the mother's advice book are intimately related to the unique means whereby it reaches out beyond itself to a less circumscribed domain. Precisely by enclosing themselves inside the domestic unit, women are enabled to step outside it and enter the marketplace of print. In developing for themselves maternal functions, these women writers strive to progress away from such a narrowly demarcated role. They are unprecedented in successfully managing to participate in religious debate while still subscribing to central places in a domestic arrangement. And, apparently addressing members of their own family, Leigh, Joscelin and their ilk broadcast to a larger audience, becoming members of a wider community. In so doing, they make a virtue of their feminine frailties and stake a claim to be heeded as salutary social observers and cultural interpreters.

CASE STUDY: ELIZABETH JOSCELIN, *THE MOTHER'S LEGACY TO HER UNBORN CHILD* (1624)

The Mother's Legacy to Her Unborn Child is elaborated as an exclusively private textual affair. Throughout, Joscelin emphasizes her secluded, closeted condition. A reader is continually reminded that the bedroom is the withdrawn environment from which the counsel originates. Thus, the work is composed 'privately in her closet between God and her[self]' (Joscelin, A9^r), with Joscelin seeing herself as a woman who is firmly

45

ensconced in a domestic sphere and who is visible only to 'the eyes of a most loving husband and a child' (*WW* 109). Intriguingly, the images offered of Joscelin after death precisely complement the representation of her in the household while still alive. If Joscelin, for instance, imagines herself lying inside the narrow walls of her tomb, her editor, Thomas Goad, locates the body not in a family grave but 'in a new sepulchre wherein was never man yet laid' (Joscelin, A9^r). Death is figured here as a continuation of Joscelin's limited and isolated life in the household, and what links the two is an emphasis upon cloistered retirement.

The seclusion of the spaces carved out by and for Joscelin is reinforced by the secrecy which surrounds the production of the narrative. Comments offered by Goad, the editor, are illuminating in this respect. He claims that only Joscelin and God knew of the text's existence during the author's lifetime and that the manuscript was discovered posthumously, concealed, appropriately, in a drawer. *The Mother's Legacy to Her Unborn Child* itself tells the same story, but goes on to construct a rationale for Joscelin having kept the manuscript a secret. Anticipating her husband's question on his discovering her writings ('thou wonderest . . . what the cause should be that . . . I should reserve this to write', *WW* 108), Joscelin provides him with an explanation that privileges her own isolated status, even within a marriage delineated as loving and intimate:

> remember how grievous it was to thee but to hear me say I may die and thou wilt confess this would have been an unpleasing discourse to thee and thou knowest I never durst displease thee willingly so much I love thee. (*WW* 108)

Paradoxically in this passage, writing becomes a gesture of obedience (it removes the death narrative from her husband's ears) and an act of love; at the same time, the potential upset of the revelation of a woman having chosen to write in the first place is minimized by the containing device of sequestration and solitude.

At several points, Joscelin stresses that she writes 'not to the world but to mine own child' (*WW* 111). The suggestion of such a familial readership is elaborated when the author reflects upon the implications of the writing act. Fearing that her feminine weakness will disallow her from executing her task, Joscelin convinces herself that she is indeed capable, if only because she writes in privacy and to her own kin; as she observes, 'I considered it was to my own ... and my love to my own might excuse my errors' (*WW* 106). Joscelin's legacy, however, is in fact addressed not simply to her child, as is the case with similar narratives, but to her unborn progeny. A contemporary consumer of her text is constantly reminded that Joscelin's offspring has not yet arrived in the world. When, as in the citation above, Joscelin speaks about writing to her 'own', therefore, this 'own' might easily be literalized as the author's own body, as her own self. In terms of privacy, Joscelin moves beyond the tropes mobilized by other writers of the genre, for she pushes the idea of the interiorized woman to its furthest extreme, confining her words not only to the boundaries of her own home but to the material accommodation of her own physicality. The idea is reinforced when Joscelin poses a hypothetical question, one which dissolves into each other the body of the mother and the form of the undelivered infant. Defending her investment in the state of her child's soul, Joscelin evokes the shared bond that makes of the mother and child a single entity, demanding: 'who would not condemn me if I should be careless of thy body while it is within me?' (*WW* 111). The blurring of child and self inside the woman's parturient body means that her address is transformed into a type of self-examination. Because she also appeals to her sense of interiority, Joscelin fashions a self-inflected discourse: the author's subjective construction of self, and the child's own corporeality, are one. At least one contemporary commentator was sensitive to the manoeuvre. In his preface, Goad, the seventeenth-century editor of *The Mother's Legacy to Her Unborn Child*, rephrases some of Joscelin's formulations, describing an author who would 'undauntedly look ... death in the face ... [yet] strangely speak ... to her own bowels' (Joscelin, A9ᵛ). Interestingly replicating a rhetorical characteristic of the narrative he presents for publication, the editor here registers a divided response. He approves a woman who shows calm before mortality and who places limitations on the circulation of her speech, yet he is more hesitant, as encapsulated in the word 'strangely', about the example of an author distinguished by a psychological communion with her bodily interstices.

That pervasive note of intimacy and privacy can be traced, too, to the legacy's absorption in the proximity of death. Unlike other mothers' advice book authors, Joscelin does not construct herself as dying as such; that is, she suffers from no illness beyond the physical discomforts that can accompany pregnancy. Rather, she writes from the position of an *anticipated* death, with her narrative looking forward to her demise as a concomitant part of giving birth. For Joscelin, then, once pregnancy has been determined, premonitions of death quickly ensue:

> I no sooner conceived a hope that I should be made a mother . . . but shortly after followed the apprehension of danger that might prevent me . . . executing that care I so exceedingly desired. (*WW* 106)

A sense of the likelihood of death permeates Joscelin's legacy, although, occasionally, her counsel rises above the inexorability of extinction to embrace the possibility that the author may live through labour and thus survive. Such moments, coloured with a tentative hope, tend to be transient and spectral, as when Joscelin addresses the unborn child 'not knowing whether I shall live to instruct thee when thou art born' (*WW* 111). They work to suggest that her narrative, composed in a fraught hiatus, operates in a limbo, in a liminal space in which all matters, including birth and death, hang in the balance. As a result, Joscelin can only once imagine the future of her legacy, should she not succumb to mortality:

> Nor shall I think this labour lost though I do live for I will make it my own looking-glass wherein to see when I am too severe, when too remiss, and in my child's fault through this glass discern mine own error, and . . . more skilfully act . . . a mother's duty. (*WW* 109)

Brief, as it is, the realization illuminates a further dimension of Joscelin's text; it demonstrates a generic connection between mothers' advice books and the diaries discussed in chapter 5, since both forms of literary endeavour provide platforms from which various forms of self-examination can be launched. But, set alongside the deathly certainties of Joscelin's sentiments, personal inspection invariably takes on a dreamy quality, precipitating in the reader no more than a sense of imminent authorial loss.

Assuming a greater prominence than self-examination in Joscelin's narrative is the continued *rhetorical pairing* of death and pregnancy. In this connection, Goad's description of pregnancy as a state of 'travelling with death' (Joscelin, A9^r) is typical. The editor contends that Joscelin secretly ordered her winding-sheet within days of first feeling her child move inside her. It is, arguably, a fanciful claim, yet it is also one that performs ideological work: the statement establishes the mutually constitutive roles of pregnancy and death while also, through its emphasis on secrecy, reinforcing the construction of the author's isolation. Unlike other mothers' advice books, which look back to labour as a means of validating the maternal voice (Leigh, for example, insistently reminds her readers of the labour experience she has survived), Joscelin's legacy looks forward to labour and imagines it as the death passage to come. Both writers see as inseparable pregnancy and pain. For Leigh, the pain is past (she 'brought [a child] forth into this world with so much bitter pain, so many groans and cries', *WW* 23); for Joscelin, the pain is yet to be experienced (she meditates upon 'so much pain as I know I must endure' to give birth and 'the painfulness of that kind of death', *WW* 109, 106). Whether adopting retrospective or prospective positions, Leigh and Joscelin associate birth with extremities of bodily suffering and physical affliction.

Linda Pollock has argued that early modern women's attitudes to childbirth were moulded by the knowledge that difficulties at birth would almost certainly lead to a painful demise.[7] Pregnant women were advised to prepare for death, chiefly through prayer, and Joscelin's ready acceptance of her likely passing might be read inside this contextual framework. In this respect, *The Mother's Legacy to Her Unborn Child* follows in the path of the earlier mother's advice book, Grymeston's *Miscellanea. Meditations. Memoratives.* This discusses in an exemplary fashion the way in which 'the woman great with child will often muse of her delivery' as 'a way to' (Grymeston, C2^v) a better life; for Grymeston, then, the heightened sensitivity of the parturient female body is a model to be imitated, providing, as it does, a strategy for confronting death 'without fear' and with 'devotion' (Grymeston, C2ᵛ). Via such formulations, the woman's body, because of its reproductive capacities, becomes a privileged explanatory site, a route to knowing and understanding redemption and salvation. It is within this interpretive frame that Goad writes glowingly of Joscelin and her preparations for meeting the deity; even though she does not die for another nine days, she asks for her funeral shroud as soon as her daughter is delivered; states the editor: 'she was made a mother of a daughter . . . she gave . . . thanks that her self had lived to see it . . . and then instantly called for her winding-sheet to be brought forth and laid upon her' (Joscelin, A9ᵛ). In this passage, the winding-sheet is constructed as replacing the pregnant body's metaphorical potential. That is, it functions similarly to the reproductive woman as a cipher for death. In the absence of a female form on the point of delivery (having given birth, Joscelin is no longer pregnant), the sheet adorning the author is transformed into an alternative instrument for a courageous *rapprochement* with mortality.

The fact that Joscelin's child is unborn additionally means that the writer cannot determine its sex. Compared to other authors utilizing the genre, therefore, Joscelin is in a unique position, since she is unable to address her legacy to one or other of the contemporary gendered constituencies. The result is that advice and recommendations in *The Mother's Legacy to Her Unborn Child*, and constructions of children, are given a sharply distinguished gendered twist. Counsel on public speech furnishes a salient example of the ways in which Joscelin conceives differently of sons and daughters and separates them out according to conventional demarcations. While 'a man ought to be careful of his speech' (*WW* 119), avoiding blasphemy, insincerity, cursing and argument, the writer maintains, a woman 'shouldst scarce speak . . . [only] if need be and yet scarcely when thou art twice asked' (*WW* 122). Advice directed at daughters, although clearer, here lacks detail; that is, while daughters are obliged to avoid only one modality of speech, sons are enjoined to resist a variety of verbal infractions. This is typical of the ways in which more complicated and nuanced prescriptions are generally reserved for sons (compared to daughters, they are the recipients of a greater volume of instructions), suggesting that Joscelin, despite appeals to womankind, packages her writing inside a patrilineal and hegemonic conception of the world. Some vices, like drunkenness, are treated as pertaining to men only, as are the more cardinal sins of irreligiosity and godly neglect: presumably, Joscelin imagines her daughter either incapable of such transgressions or lacking the opportunity to indulge. By contrast, vanity and inordinate fashion are seen as failings common to both sexes, although a daughter is judged more susceptible 'because thou art weaker and thy temptations to this vice greater' (*WW* 115). Interestingly, this is one of the few occasions on which daughters receive fuller instruction: while daughters are given 'leave to follow modest fashions but not to be a beginner of fashions' (*WW* 116), sons are encouraged to abstain from fashion altogether. Despite the absence of a delivered child, Joscelin still betrays the orientation of her gendered allegiances, biases and balances that imitate the division of men and women within the contemporary order. Once again, however, a seeming endorsement of seventeenth-century orthodoxies belies the reality of Joscelin's achievement. For the discovery of a 'scarce' speaking daughter is in tension with Joscelin's own status as a fully writing subject, and the prospect of a modestly dressed woman sits uneasily alongside an author who, putting herself into print, makes of her own body and experience a visual and textual spectacle.

Even at the level of tone, moreover, marked differences still obtain. While Joscelin almost always addresses a son directly, appealing to him as 'thou' or 'thee', advice to a daughter is channelled through her husband: it is the husband who is responsible for ensuring the regularity of the daughter's behaviour. The deployment of the spouse as a conduit suggests that daughters, in comparison to sons, are conceived of as inferior guardians of their own conduct. Yet deferential privileging of the husband runs against the grain of Joscelin's more general comments on daughterly upbringing. The certainty, tightness and precision of her recommendations for the rearing of daughters suggest confidence and knowledge, the effect of which is to undercut the positioning of the husband in a go-between capacity.

A similar paradox is encapsulated in the discussion of female education. Despite her own experience (Goad notes that

Joscelin boasted an impressive learning), the author recommends for her daughter a narrower schooling than her own; with such counsel articulated, she modulates into a discussion of the education of women in general:

> I desire her bringing up may be learning the Bible ... good housewifery, writing and good works: other learning a woman needs not, though I admire it in those whom God hath blessed with discretion, yet I desire it not much in my own, having seen that sometimes women have greater portions of learning than wisdom, which is of no better use to them than a mainsail to a fly-boat, which runs it under water. But where learning and wisdom meet in a virtuous disposed woman, she is the fittest closet for all goodness. She is like a well-balanced ship, that may bear all her sail. (*WW* 107)

Valerie Wayne has drawn attention to the conflicting uses of the metaphors of 'closet' and 'ship' here. Joscelin claims that women who tie their education to the home (the closet) resemble a 'well-balanced ship', but, as Wayne argues, 'her choice of tropes betrays her own ambivalence toward confinement ... The very language she uses enacts a transgression of the norms she is supposedly advocating'.[8] More broadly, Joscelin presents us with the phenomenon of an educated woman in the same moment as she opposes women who have benefited from education, with the very existence of her narrative working against her own ostensible views. In short, the legacy that Joscelin furnishes is a vexed and uneven gift, one that simultaneously celebrates female production and publication and moves repressively against women's authorial activities. The conservative tendencies implicit in Joscelin's *The Mother's Legacy to Her Unborn Child* are at odds with the textual strategies the author has deployed to bring herself before the public gaze. These discontinuities are typical of the genre of the mother's advice book; they also point to the unstable locations of seventeenth-century women themselves, as they looked to define themselves in relation to embattled ideological polarities.

4

Prophecy

GENRE, RANGE, WRITERS

In January 1654, Anna Trapnel first came to public notice. Attending the examination of Vavasor Powell, the Baptist preacher at Whitehall, Trapnel effectively stole his spotlight by falling into a twelve-day trance. Crowds came to view this extraordinary spiritual spectacle, to witness the authenticity of Trapnel's state and to listen to her rhyming, singing speech, recorded at the time by a colleague and published in the same year as *The Cry of a Stone* and *Strange and Wonderful News from Whitehall*. Unsurprisingly, such activities swiftly brought this shipwright's daughter to the attention of the local authorities. Later that year, when Trapnel travelled to Cornwall on behalf of her church, she found her missionary zeal rewarded with imprisonment in London's notorious Bridewell. An account of this experience forms the basis of *Anna Trapnel's Report* (1654). *A Legacy for Saints* (also 1654), a compilation of further visions, followed soon afterwards, while a slightly later text, *A Voice for the King of Saints* (1658), completes Trapnel's *oeuvre*, solidifying her place as a public, prolific and politically engaged female author.

This colourful narrative of textual inception – at some remove from our perception of the author as a figure privately scribbling in a lonely attic – has proved attractive to those popular biographers who have settled on Trapnel as an extraordinary individual. However, it is important to remember that, in her authorship of prophetic texts, Trapnel was only one of a number of women who deployed the form over the course of the seventeenth century. Equally productive, among others, were Lady Eleanor Douglas and Jane Lead: *The New Jerusalem at Hand* (1649) and *The Revelation of Revelations* (1683) provide respective examples of their work. Indeed, Patricia Crawford's checklist of seventeenth-century women's published writings demonstrates that more than half of publications by women during the period could be deemed 'prophetic'.[1] In the middle decades of the century, with the growth in sectarian activity accompanying a widespread millennial anxiety, the prophetic form was particularly prominent. Although there are still examples circulating at the end of the 1690s, prophetic activity tailed off after the Restoration, due, mainly, to greater governmental control over sectarian affairs. The wealth of prophetic material authored by women across the century, therefore, takes us away from the construction of individual prophets as isolated figures and towards an understanding of prophetic identity as crucial for any broad assessment of seventeenth-century female literary output.

Any such assessment must begin with a historicized understanding of the term 'prophecy' itself. We tend to understand prophecy anachronistically, as a seeing into the future, but, as Diane Purkiss has argued, 'in the seventeenth century, prophecy was any utterance produced by God through human agency'.[2] Here Purkiss downplays the notion that the defining quality of prophecy is that it foretells the future; instead, she focuses attention on the basis of the speech act. 'Prophecy', then, need not restrict itself to visions but might include as well other sorts of discourse, on the condition that they are divinely inspired. Trapnel's *Report* is typical of most prophetic texts and stands, in fact, as a hybrid creation, since accounts of visions unfold in conjunction with autobiography and self-defence, prayers, dramatic interludes and poetry, and passages of moral exhortation and political critique. In the same vein, even Elinor Channel's brief work, *A Message from God by a Dumb Woman* (1654), finds time to mix mystical insights with recommendations for the ordering of society and a record of private domestic circumstances. Running through the prophetic text is a need to establish the divine origins of the speaking voice, and this is registered in the form's characteristic denials of authorship. Channel, for example, refers to 'an audible voice' telling her 'how to express her message from

God', while Trapnel impatiently rejects a charge of agency in relation to her *The Cry of a Stone*: 'There is no self in this thing', she insists.[3] A characteristic relegation of the author and a concomitant elevation of divine influence were obviously vital in establishing a legitimized articulacy. But these strategies also offered an implicit rejoinder to prohibitions against women's speech and writing, for if the woman author was merely a conduit, and the text was 'in fact' authored by a God gendered male, on what grounds could detractors reasonably object?

Logic of this kind was given an additional boost in that seventeenth-century women were considered to be particularly suitable for acting as mediums for divine messages. Phyllis Mack, in particular, has suggested that because women in the period were constructed as emotional, irrational and receptive to external influences, they were obvious candidates for disseminating the holy word.[4] Mack's thesis begins to point to the ways in which mid-century women were able to mobilize stereotypes in order to fashion a powerful speaking voice and negotiate a route into print. Her arguments have been elaborated by critics such as Sue Wiseman, who, taking Mary Cary as a key instance, claims that utilizing conventional stereotypes of femininity functions 'to establish as much as possible the typological, historical, spiritual and factual veracity' of the prophetic visions which ensue.[5] Crucially, Wiseman contends, Cary is careful to position herself in the preface to her *The Little Horn's Doom* (1651) as 'a weak and unworthy instrument' with no 'strength of [her] own'.[6] The example thus illustrates the ways in which this particular genre at this critical historical moment allows a female writer to capitalize upon contemporary constructions of femininity in order to perform individual authorial work.

Implicit in Wiseman's argument is the acknowledgement that prophetic texts are usually written according to a purpose. That is, they constitute documents circulating in the public domain and are directed towards achieving a specific effect. Much of the detailed significances of women's prophetic visions have yet to be teased out. However, research conducted thus far has played a vital part in establishing the connections between prophetic roles and political intervention, illuminating women's vibrant participation in contemporary politics, an arena from which they were traditionally thought to have been excluded. A locally informed reading of the prophetic texts of Cary and Channel, for example, reveals them to be deeply involved in, among other things, central debates about the execution of Charles I, the establishment of the Protectorate, the distribution of wealth, the treatment of debtors and the role and responsibilities of the army. The contrasting politics of the women writing – and it is important to bear in mind that prophetic authors span the whole range of Protestantism as well as an extensive spectrum of opinion in relation to the English Civil War – often present a lively picture of conflict and intervention. Nor are subjects and allegiances necessarily predictable in terms of religious and class connections. Hence, the targets of the aristocratic Lady Eleanor Douglas embrace Charles I, while Trapnel (who was closely associated with the revolutionary impetus of the Fifth Monarchist millennial movement) rails bitterly against the growing power of Oliver Cromwell. As the case study below will suggest, the rationale for such seeming anomalies can be pinpointed through a process of close contextualization, which does not simply set women's prophecies against broad political alliances but reads them inside minute yet complex historical moments of production and reception.

The ways in which prophetic women enunciate their politics, moreover, are often as revealing as the actual content. Textual vacillations between the politics of state and the politics of the family in the mid-seventeenth-century utterances of, say, Elizabeth Poole, may be in line with the dominance of family–state analogies at this time; nevertheless, when detected in female-authored work, such inconsistencies illuminate both how women imagined their domestic and private lives and how sectarian activity impacted upon the domestic unit. Equally intriguing is the extent to which the prophetic genre seems to have lent itself to the use of domestic metaphors, with prophetesses frequently drawing on female experiences of virginity, childbirth, lactation, child-rearing and familial sustenance. These realms of activity belong with what Diane Purkiss has described as the 'bodily visibility'[7] of the female prophet: as the defining symbol of the authenticity of her prophecy, the prophetess' body is always to the fore. The prophetic genre's conventional inclusion of illness, trembling, fainting and bodily incapacity – all of which were characterized in the seventeenth century as specifically female – also contributes to this corporeal modality. On occasions, the process takes on a material guise, as this chapter's opening anecdote about Trapnel shows: her body, incapacitated by a trance-like state, was openly displayed. A corporeal focus is further glimpsed in the text's corresponding physicality. Many prophetic texts exhibit an obsession with blood and bodily pain, which extends to menstruation, labour and even self-harm. Material or metaphorical, the public corporeality of the prophetess runs contrary to contemporary notions of female privacy, illuminating prophecy as a site where the territory between public and private is fraught with indistinction.

Other types of slippage feature forcefully in the prophetic text. One of the most striking concerns the shifting ground prophetic discourse occupies with madness, possession, magic and witchcraft. Ascriptions of 'insanity' are often conferred on the female prophetic utterance. Thus, in a tellingly anxious articulation, Trapnel reflects upon the refusal to recognize her divine inspiration: 'England's rulers and clergy do judge the Lord's handmaid to be mad, and under the administration of evil angels, and a witch'.[8] The misinterpretation of the prophetic voice carried with it potentially life-threatening social consequences: Lady Eleanor Douglas was confined to Bedlam, while Trapnel herself was tried for witchcraft. More importantly, the moment when one mode of being blurs into, or is confused with, another brings us back to the connection (central to any autobiographically oriented articulation) between life and text. When a printed page is initially orally generated (for example, via a trance-like speech, as in Trapnel's case) and then transcribed (either at the time or on a subsequent occasion) by a listener or an interlocutor, there are obvious implications for the 'I' of the account. Questions about whether the voice delineated in Trapnel's prophecies belongs to her, her scribe or her church immediately spring to mind here, as does the problem of how we might assimilate the fact that the speaking subject arrives at several removes from an 'original'. In other words, it is vital to cogitate cautiously upon the parts played variously and often simultaneously by amanuensis, author, woman prophetess and scribe.

CASE STUDY: ANNA TRAPNEL, *ANNA TRAPNEL'S REPORT* (1654)

It may not be accidental that four out of six of the Trapnel texts were published in 1654, a year when the Fifth Monarchists found themselves out of favour. Just six months earlier, members of this political movement had occupied the centre of the political stage. In April 1653, Cromwell's Barebones Parliament included in its 140 members a dozen Fifth Monarchists, making them a significant presence at the heart of the political nation. Many of their views enjoyed a widespread currency, with even Cromwell himself, as Peter Gaunt states, seeming 'to share many' Fifth Monarchist 'millenarian assumptions'.[9] To contemporaries it must have seemed as if the millenarian tendency had reached the zenith point of its influence. But, by December, parliament had been dissolved; the army had resumed power; and a crackdown on the Fifth Monarchist movement had been instituted. Major leaders were imprisoned, and a campaign of counter-propaganda resulted not only in a tide of anti-Fifth Monarchical sentiment but also in a loss of crucial popular support.

The transformation in the Monarchists' fortunes is encapsulated in one of Trapnel's most evocative visions. In this unsettlingly inspired fantasy, Cromwell metamorphoses from a 'Gideon' figure, 'going before Israel, blowing the trumpet of courage and valour', to a bull, charging 'at many precious saints that stood in the way of him, that looked boldly in his face' (CS 6, 13). Neatly drawn in Trapnel's phrasing is the Monarchists' sense of betrayal, since her characterization of Cromwell as 'Gideon' recalls the terms with which Fifth Monarchists had previously greeted him as leader and emphasizes a conviction that their ousting from power had been an abuse of trust. Courage, at first the preserve of the parliamentary hero, migrates to inhabit instead the souls of the saints, thereby discovering the descent of Cromwell from human to animal, the replacement of his saving graces by an irrational

58

rage, and the shift in his role, from leader, who can be relied upon, to destroyer, who must be actively confronted. The saint's part, it seems, in the wake of the devastation wrought by the bull, is to promote the virtue of passive resistance.

There are intriguing correspondences between this perception of saintly strength and Trapnel's stance, towards the climax of the *Report*, when she is tried as a witch. At this point, the author represents herself set against huge powers, such as the 'sessions house' holders of constituted authority ('justices', 'lawyers' and 'clergymen') and the 'witch-trying woman', all bent upon convicting the prophetess herself (*R.* 24). Notably, Trapnel's decision not to buckle is most fully realized not so much through what she says as via her self-conscious adoption of an appropriate 'posture' – that is, she constructs herself looking 'boldly' into her prosecutors' faces (*R.* 24). The language in which this fearless encounter is described echoes that deployed in the reading of the saints' valiant resolve before the bull's onslaught, suggesting, perhaps, that for the female prophetess, confrontation (even against insuperable odds) is the only possible response to the arbitrary actions of state-sanctioned power.

At a deeper level, the figures of the saint and the bull form a connection with the defensive positions, and contrary mechanisms, that energize Trapnel's *Report* as a whole. From the outset, her account is located within an oppositional framework. The title page describes the *Report* as 'a defiance', and linguistic patterns constantly return to this idea by revealing Trapnel in antithetical situations: she invariably uses the word 'against' to conceptualize her writing's broader functions. Through its politics of negativity, the text appears as a challenging rebuttal, a narrative that will be at odds with a dominant mindset. We find this reading confirmed in the text's constant evocation of what it is pitched against. Much of Trapnel's polemic is aimed at what she regards as the coercive force and destructive power of 'false rumour', 'reports . . . very contrary' and 'false accusations' (*R.* 15). Purposefully interrogative of this weight of accusation, the narrative frequently dramatizes episodes where rumours betray themselves as insubstantial. Typically, Trapnel represents herself dissolving misinformation with an oral version of her life story. On arrival in Cornwall, for example, the author meets some doubters who, 'having been informed before concerning my spirit', hardened their 'hearts . . . against me'. Initial resistance notwithstanding, the suspicious group, having appreciated the articulation of Trapnel's self-image, 'became loving friends' (*R.* 11). The life story adumbrated here is imbued with a creative power, one which can dispel misleading murmurs, alter assumptions, change minds and win hearts.

In many ways, these and similar transformations are set in place as examples, as oral versions of the mental movement that the reader of the *Report* is encouraged to pursue throughout. Just as knowledge gained from the prophetess' own mouth is encapsulated in the episode above as altering perception and promoting verity, so is the *Report* oriented towards the fulfilment of a comparable change in readerly consciousness. According to Trapnel, 'the reader' of 'the ensuing discourse' will be moved to 'understand the malice . . . uttered and acted . . . against me' (*R.* A2^r) and thus, by implication, to know the 'truth'.

Because Trapnel's subject has an intimate dimension, because she writes in relation to an 'I' and because her 'truth' emerges through the autobiographical relation, one could be forgiven for thinking that the 'truth' in question bears directly upon the author's own life. In this context, the peculiarly emphatic rejection of the slanders laid at her door suggests that Trapnel's account has as its imperative a will to clear the author's own name. However, Trapnel is careful, at the beginning of the *Report*, to rule out such a possibility: 'I go not about to vindicate myself, but the truth . . . the Lord knows, I would not reach out tongue, hand nor pen, to right my self, or to seek restoration of my loss' (*R.* A1^{r-v}). The editors of the anthology *Her Own Life: Autobiographical Writings by Seventeenth-Century Englishwomen* argue that, in these opening lines, Trapnel sets the 'truth of God's word . . . in opposition to her ''self''; the former is dependent on the absence of the latter'.[10] But this denial of the self, combined with the constant intrusion of the 'I' and the predilection for 'vindication', suggest that Trapnel's antithetical balancing-act is more complicated. Instead of substituting one property for another, Trapnel at this point, I would argue, brings the self and God's 'truth' into dramatic alignment. By putting the two into play

60

together (the 'truth' is validated through the life story), Trapnel positions her life story inside a divine paradigm or, more precisely, inside the doctrinal framework of the Fifth Monarchists themselves. Rather than simply obliterating the self, the passage reveals Trapnel encapsulating a personal history within the broader 'life' of a political narrative.

The title page forcibly advertises such a movement, literalizing the mobility that the rest of the narrative celebrates. Here we find the *Report* described in the same moment as 'a narrative of [Trapnel's] journey from London' *and* as a proclamation about 'the rage and strivings of the people against the comings forth of the Lord Jesus to reign; manifested in the harsh, rough, boisterous, rugged, inhumane and uncivil usage of Anna Trapnel, by the justices and people in Cornwall'. The misused, abused and imprisoned body of Trapnel becomes a metaphor for, or a 'manifestation' of, what the Fifth Monarchist believes to be the pervading state of England's myopia and denial. Trapnel's autobiography is imagined as valuable for its metaphoric potential, for its capacity to figure in its contours a more extended story of political injustice. Inside this reading, the false reports that Trapnel is keen to obliterate through the autobiographical rehearsal of the *Report* touch not so much upon her *per se* as they do upon the Fifth Monarchist phenomenon in its entirety.

Nowhere is such a political identification explicitly made, although one might argue that, at several points, it is excitingly implicit. For example, in the careful registration of previous visitors at the places where she stops en route to Cornwall, it is possible to see Trapnel both carving out for herself a niche in a developing tradition and stressing the similarity of her life pattern to that of other group members. More revealing still are the references Trapnel makes to 'friends' or other church members who have experienced or are currently suffering similar experiences to her own. In this regard, Trapnel's brief reference to visits to 'Tower-friends' (*R*. 6) operates to foster a sense of the typicality of her predicament. Because of the dangerous implications of their agitations, many contemporary Fifth Monarchists were subjected to periods of imprisonment. So frequent and unspecific is Trapnel's evocation of an imprisoned collective that the experience of gaol appears as a shaping context for the narrative, one which simultaneously bonds Trapnel to others and foregrounds the ways in which her own history will culminate. Via these and similar comments and insertions, the author succeeds in constructing a picture of an organization whose members' lives mirror hers, whose stories echo her own progress. Furthermore, the process functions in a reciprocal manner. In the same way that Trapnel's situation casts light on the plight of various prisoners, so do their predicaments illuminate her own. Thus, in her obvious connection to these unfortunates, and in the courageous terms deployed to delineate them, Trapnel implicitly instructs her readers in the art of how properly to view her subsequent sojourn at Her Majesty's pleasure. The virtues accorded to other Fifth Monarchists shine back on Trapnel, who is briefly and individually illuminated.

The impression that Trapnel's story works no less importantly as the narrative of a congregation is vividly realized in the leave-taking scene. In general over the course of the seventeenth century, sectarian women seem to have sought and found sustenance among 'communities' of similarly minded believers. Trapnel's *Report* represents a salient acting-out of these kinds of support mechanisms, since the prophetess' proximity to her fellows is highlighted through narrative linkages between her own behaviour and the sect's praying practices. A network of correspondences joins to construct Trapnel's visions as phenomena emanating from, and belonging to, church members. Significantly, recollections that Trapnel is in others' thoughts are causally inserted before almost every narrative climax, reinforcing the notion that church members, however far-flung, can guide the author's conduct. The mutual interplay between supporters' thoughts and Trapnel's conduct is reinforced in the text's frequent alternation between the 'I' and 'we' forms, and in its emphasis on recording gratitude for material, as well as spiritual, backing. Each congregation, via its multivalent provisions of aid, is shown to be exemplary in an individually focused dynamics of influence, positing the Fifth Monarchy movement as a whole as the determining power behind Trapnel's throne.

In its broad locations of the prophetess' voice, in its barely suppressed history of persecution and in its revelation of the metaphorical tenor of the protagonist's experience, the *Report* declares itself a sophisticated work of propaganda, a testimony with the potential to alter public perception. Crucial to its meanderings, of course, are the responses of its readers. As the editors of *Her Own Life* suggest, the title alone points to the fact that the account 'should not only record, but also persuade: it is a "plea" as well as a "report" ',[11] a conflated production which necessitates a reader's active involvement. Throughout, the reader is enjoined to 'judge' and to 'weigh' (*R*. A3^r) the text's contents, becoming, in the process, an interpretive unit of the narrative and a working component in the production of its overall effects. And, while the prophetess may address her implied reader as singular, she conceives of this textual participant as belonging to large and disparate groupings. In terms of their spiritual affiliation, these individuals may be 'obedient to . . . the Lord . . . or yet in the dark' (*R*. A3^r). As far as their geographical and class locations are concerned, those the author appeals to comprise all 'sorts of people, high and low . . . in all parts' (*R*. A3^r). Trapnel has in mind, then, a generalized readership, a textually sensitive population ripe for reformation of belief and conversion to the millenarian dream.

Given the construction of a broad readership, it is not surprising that Trapnel takes care to situate herself in a sympathetic light. In common with other writers of the period, Trapnel exhibits an acute consciousness of her gendered status and of the requirement to conform to cultural norms of feminine behaviour. The fashioning effect that this imperative has on the narrative is everywhere apparent, perhaps nowhere more obviously than in the author's ready acknowledgement of the inappropriate nature of her spiritually clairvoyant duties. The prophetess records her response to her first calling as a respectable revulsion against 'this public-spiritedness' (*R*. 17), and makes a point of positing silence as both her 'natural' and her preferred state. A shrewd distinction is drawn between her normative condition and her in-trance state on describing a visit to a family 'before whom I thought myself unfit to speak, when I was in an ordinary capacity; but being filled extraordinarily, I wanted not words . . . and learning' (*R*. 5). In 'ordinary' state, Trapnel is silent, uneducated and self-conscious; in 'extraordinary' state, she is voluble, learned and didactic. The contrast between the two subject positions inhabited here deflates a possible anti-feminine objection, placing the focus instead on the divine inspiration that can make Trapnel God's expressively chosen mechanism.

More broadly, that spectre of negative gendered assumption is shadowed in Trapnel's investment in self-effacement. Even when discovering herself at the centre of the action, Trapnel is quick simultaneously to effect her remove: she executes this manoeuvre by placing affirmation in the mouths of others and by casting herself, as did many women writers of the period, as a worm. Thus, on leaving Plymouth to travel to London's Bridewell, she writes that many people 'were sorry to have me go from their quarters, not that I was anything, but the Lord did their souls good through a worm' (R. 34–5). Casual remarks about her own insignificance find theoretical support in longer, more elaborate passages, which stress an assumed divine tendency to invert conventional power dynamics. In a topsy turvy vision, Trapnel focuses on a passage from 1 Corinthians (1:27–8):

> God hath chosen the foolish things . . . to confound the wise and . . . the weak things . . . to confound the . . . mighty; and base things of the world, and things which are despised, hath God chosen . . . to bring to nought things that are . . . I could be contented to be made use of under these terms . . . (R. 17)

Via a debasement of the self, Trapnel stakes a claim to God-given authority and divinely approved agency.

The creation of a receptive readerly audience depends, too, on emphases and omissions that, reconfiguring key events and experiences, help to promote a Fifth Monarchist propagandist paradigm. Trapnel's denial of volition, for example, begins long before the relation of her Cornish crisis. The opening of the *Report* posits a Trapnel unwilling to travel to the county: 'I would pray against going to Cornwall . . . my mind was so strongly bent against the journey' (R. 1), she states. God is seen as going to great lengths to enforce the rightness of the author's transmigratory task, causing her to become ill and granting her a vision of the experience (R. 3, 5). The subsequent elaboration of a friendless environment, of a daunting journey, of physical interventions and of divine visitations – all help to fashion Trapnel as a resisting representative.

Entering Cornwall, the prophetess is keen to put a distance between herself and the rapid acceleration of events which culminate in her arrest and extradition. Of course, it is possible to speculate that Trapnel and her supporters themselves encouraged controversy through spontaneously staging visions which, because public and prolonged, offered a threat to existing hierarchical arrangements. However, Trapnel is sufficiently circumspect to deny her own determining influence in disturbance. While she pauses to register the throng about her house, for instance, Trapnel expresses surprise that the same mass of curiosity-seekers turns up at the courthouse: 'I was amazed to see so many people' (R. 28). The familiar rhetorical gesture elides a perception of Trapnel as a mistress of publicity with the confirmation that constituted authority is a body to be discountenanced. Similarly, Trapnel's careful delineation of her physical condition at this time – the judges 'caused my eyelids to be pulled up for they said I held them fast, because I would deceive the people' (R. 21) – steers a sure course between personal conviction and exterior rationalism, perhaps anticipating the objections of readers more sceptical of prophetic authenticity.

While these episodes have as their immediate rationale an urge to undo rumours of sedition and malpractice, they also have a deeper purpose. The evocation of a specular and examinatory judiciary ties Trapnel's prosecutors to shadowy figures who, patrolling the periphery of the narrative, subject her to surveillance. Both random comments and explicit asides discover a Trapnel who is under constant scrutiny. Phrases such as 'many watched what [was] said in prayer' (R. 22), and 'there were listeners under the window' (R. 22), are embellishments to an environment in which policing and monitoring are the norms. It is as if Trapnel inhabits a world populated by the seventeenth-century equivalent of invasive modern photographers – eager for a story and bent upon securing discredit.

At the author's entrance to Cornwall, for example, Trapnel is impelled to imagine a threatening underside to her otherwise warm welcome: 'They frowningly and dissemblingly saluted me, though their hearts were against me . . . it made me very thoughtful what it would produce' (*R.* 11). In encouraging readers to build bridges between represented present and narrative future, and in promoting a perception of gaps between external behaviours and inner motivations, Trapnel appropriates at this point, as at others, an essentially novelistic mode of suspense. It can hardly be accidental that this scene is immediately followed by one of the lengthy transcribed dialogues with God, in which he insists that, to bring the divine plan to fruition, Trapnel must 'suffer many ways' (*R.* 12). The artful juxtaposition of the divine communion and the doubting personalities urges speculation about the specific form of Trapnel's forthcoming suffering. Not only will the tribulations to ensue be ordained by Trapnel's heavenly conversationalist, the narrative suggests: they will also take the form of a species of martyrdom.

The construction of the author as a martyr is resumed again in the comparable emphasis placed on Trapnel's appalling prison environment and refusal to petition for release. Long descriptive passages are devoted to describing the conditions in Bridewell: 'difficulties to undergo night and day' include the 'cold' and 'damp', the 'grievous' smell of the air, 'rats' and 'scolding among the prisoners' (*R.* 40, 43, 44), all of which serve to locate the incapacitating illness from which Trapnel suffers – the gaol is the 'cause of my sickness' (*R.* 40–43). Growing out of the martyr-like image of Trapnel is the paralleling of her story and Christ's career. The trials of conversation with two unsavoury Bridewell inmates give rise to consolatory reflections upon the 'saviour as he was hung between two thieves' (*R.* 40), and, at this moment, Trapnel and Christ consort in a clear analogy.

Moreover, in structural terms, it is tempting to see the latter half of the *Report* as directly indebted to the Passion narrative, because the conversion by Christ of the Roman soldier who witnesses his crucifixion chimes with Trapnel's conversion of the soldier who escorts her from Cornwall to London (*R.* 27). By the same token, Trapnel, like Christ, refuses to agitate for liberty, despite being capable of securing emancipation:

> Some came and desired me to petition, I told them I had not offended any, whereby to seek to him . . . some others came and

said, they knew they could quickly procure my liberty; I told them I would not come out upon base terms . . . but suffer imprisonment. (*R*. 45–6)

The ultimate indication of the constructed nature of Trapnel's martyrdom comes at the point where freedom is finally awarded. Because no clear explanation for the suspension of the gaol sentence is provided, the narrative is able to suggest an official acknowledgement of the prejudice and persecution that, meted out to a movement, are also inscribed on the body of Trapnel herself. The closing pages of the *Report* stage and reinforce the integral connections between the microcosmic sense of self and the macrocosmic conception of Trapnel's political affiliation, and the narrative ends with a forceful repudiation of the suggestion that the author, despite her relation of suffering, has found in prison some benefit:

> That day, I spoke to some that said he would choose imprisonment for . . . outward gain . . . I am sure I cannot say, nor those that are imprisoned upon this account for the Fifth Monarchy, cannot say so: we would not gain for our outward man [even] if we might. (*R*. 47)

In its denial that gain can be gleaned from imprisonment, Trapnel's 'I' acquires strength and dominion as it shifts inexorably into the company of the 'we'. The ease of the transition stands as testimony to the ground that the narrative has covered. It is hardly coincidental that the considered self-imaginings of the *Report* are followed, within the text, by the expressive invective of 'A Defiance to All Reproachful, Scandalous, Base, Horrid, Defaming Speeches . . . Vented by Rulers, Clergy and Their Auditors' (*R*. 49). The new language offered here, and the unprecedented tone that the 'defiance' displays, are made possible only because of the intricate negotiations that have come before. And, when Trapnel demands that the reader 'labour to amend' previous misunderstandings of the Fifth Monarchy through the articulation of 'candid and charitable constructions' (*R*. 59), she speaks from a position that the autobiographical narrative of her life has been central in creating.

5

Diaries and Memoirs

GENRE, RANGE, WRITERS

In terms of studying women's lives and histories, diaries and memoirs enjoy a significant potential. For the first-person narrative represents an unparalleled inscription of the private, domestic activities of the seventeenth-century female; at the same time, it helps us to understand the ways in which contemporary women's domestic roles could extend into, and be restrained by, the public sphere. More generally, diaries and memoirs provide a sense of how the seventeenth-century woman imagined herself and articulated her relation to dominant social and cultural expectations. Thus, as well as yielding glimpses into a woman's quotidian practices, these neglected literary forms are vital in establishing the broader contexts that shaped the seventeenth-century woman's existence.

For the majority of writers of diaries and memoirs, the impetus to write was devotional. Most diaries and memoirs produced in the seventeenth century seem to have been initiated out of the need to record, and even enforce, a religious routine. Hence, the emphasis is on recording prayers, attendance at sermons and other religious duties, although most diaries also commemorate a domestic order which includes household organization, child-bearing and rearing, and work undertaken in the local community (such as nursing and charity provision). An extract from the diary of Lady Margaret Hoby, which was maintained between 1599 and 1605, offers a forceful registration of this spiritual ethos:

After private prayers I did eat my breakfast and then went to church: after, I came home and prayed, then I dined and, when I had talked a while with some of my neighbours, I went again to church: and, after the sermon, I went about the house and took order for diverse things which were to be done in my absence, and, at five o'clock, I returned to private prayer and meditation. After I went to supper, then to lector [reading], and so to bed.[1]

Despite the nature of Hoby's activities, and her investment in regulating domestic affairs in accordance with spiritual discipline, her diary represents an essentially flat reading experience. The prose is unadorned and stark, the entry structured in such a way as to highlight religious exercises and to privilege the position of a woman whose daily expectations are rigorously godly. The continual documenting of spiritual business, invariably using the same phrasing and syntax, can appear monotonous and suggestive of a lack of personal reflection or involvement. There is little of what we might recognize as the diary's expected self-analysis, and what introspection can be detected is generally in the form of prayer or confession. For example, the previous entry to the extract above mentions a Bible-reading meeting 'where many sundry distractions withdrew my mind from so profitable hearing as I ought':[2] here, the brief insight into Hoby's psychological state is both enabled by, and contained within, a spiritual frame of reference. In the same way, a later seventeenth-century diary by Mary Rich, begun shortly after the Restoration, seems, on initial inspection, to communicate little more than an everyday sense of the writer's circumscribed conditions and confined conformities. For Rich as for Hoby, the writing style is bare and unpolished, leading to predictable readerly effects. The case study of this chapter, however, argues that, while a repetitive writing style is typical of a diary intended for private use, this constrains neither the critic's role nor interpretive possibilities. Contrary to the initial impressions created by seventeenth-century female diaries, the chapter contends that, by attending to linguistic habits, syntactical arrangements and recurring motifs, a lively and important recovery of a contemporary woman can be attempted.

Unearthing patterns of significance in the seemingly uncommunicative conventions of the diary has a precedent in the early modern period. We know that some women diarists destroyed their manuscripts to prevent posthumous exposure, suggesting a sensitivity about the revelation of the content of their work. Other diarists took steps, through mobilizing a personally encripted shorthand, to conceal their thoughts and reflections from prying eyes. Elizabeth Bury of Clare, Suffolk, who maintained a spiritual diary from *c.* 1690 to 1720, is a case in point. By ensuring shorthand entries, she was able to forestall her husband's scrutiny; as he stated after her death, 'her accounts . . . cannot be recovered by me . . . because of many peculiar characters and abbreviations of her own'.[3] It is also possible that manuscripts were disposed of by family members who found the subject matter objectionable: Samuel Pepys' destruction of his wife's diary is an infamous example. By virtue of its personal connections and private field of circulation, then, the diary form stands as an implicitly transient writing medium. In fact, Sara Heller Mendelson, while acknowledging 'the real importance of religion in the lives of seventeenth-century women' in her overview of twenty-three Stuart female diaries and occasional memoirs, argues that it 'is probably no accident that three-quarters of the works in the present sample contain considerable devotional content. Feminine piety always reflected well upon the family, and any tangible display of it might be considered sufficiently edifying to preserve'.[4] To compose a spiritually oriented diary was to engage with an approved mechanism for ordering daily life; it may also have been to seize upon the most likely route to permanency and, subsequently, publication.

Although they form a minority of extant texts, some diaries, including those of Lady Anne Clifford, Countess of Pembroke, are motivated by a more secular desire to establish a record of an individual woman's life and achievements. Maintaining a diary on-and-off from 1603 onwards (she died in 1676), Clifford is unusual in that her entries regularly move beyond the domestic and the day-to-day to describe her infringement of the public, and masculine, arena of the law. (Notable in this connection is Clifford's long-running duel with James I over her legal entitlement to her family Westmorland estates.) The highly wrought diary, with its reliance upon secular self-justification, may present an absorbing intellectual prospect, but, as later sections of this chapter will show, it did not necessarily convey a more contestatory female subjectivity nor did it represent the end-point of women's interventions in the genre.

In its structured appearance, Clifford's diary forms a bridge to the more episodic format adopted in memoirs. Once again, few memoirs surviving from the seventeenth century seem to have been written with publication in mind: Margaret Cavendish's *A True Relation of My Birth, Breeding and Life*, first published in 1656, is an exception to the rule. Few, if any, seventeenth-century women would argue, as did Cavendish, that their writing was generated from ambition and from a desire 'to live by remembrance in after-ages'.[5] Rather, as with diaries, most extant memoirs can be traced to a devotional imperative. Hence, Alice Thornton's 'Book of Remembrances' of *c*. 1668 is one of many contemporary female reminiscences informed by the narrative of God's mercies to the author. The 'Book' announces itself as an account of God's providential dealings, which are revealed in the 'remarkable deliverances' of herself, her husband and children.[6] An incongruous summary, which sits uneasily alongside the gloomy timbre of the autobiography as a whole, is evident here, yet it is still one that clarifies the powerful presence of religion in the female self-authoring enterprise.

A stated aim of religious self-justification notwithstanding, seventeenth-century women's memoirs are often novelistic in tendency; they appeal immediately to the modern reader and share strategic similarities with the prose fictions examined in chapter 7. *The Memoirs of Anne, Lady Halkett*, dating from 1677 to 1678, are perhaps the most striking of these fiction-suffused productions. Halkett's tales of love and honour, which are set against a backdrop of Royalist defeat in the Civil War, are cogently structured and felicitously narrated, employing such novelistic devices as direct addresses to the reader, episodic developments and suspense. Such memoirs tend to be written with an audience in mind, although the interested party may have been not a general consumer but a member of the author's own family. In other memoirs of the period, the impulse to textual transmission is, indeed, explicitly framed in familial or generational terms.

If some memoirs employ strategies more commonly associated with the novel, others take on qualities that share a greater affinity with the biography. Lady Ann Fanshawe's manuscript memoirs, composed in 1676 and addressed to her son, comprise 'actions and accidents . . . of your father and my life'.[7] The memoir records Fanshawe's life with the statesman, Sir Richard Fanshawe, who worked for the return of Charles II and who briefly held the post of ambassador to Madrid. Once married, women legally became a part of their husbands' property, and therefore it is not surprising that, for many women, the projects of writing their autobiographies and compiling the biographies of their spouses were intimately connected. The work of Theodosia Alleine is pertinent here. Writing the biography of her dissident husband in 1671, she provides ample testimony of the ways in which his experience jeopardizes her own internal and external stability. A prison sentence for him means a prison sentence for her, quite literally, as Alleine makes clear in a passage describing the tension they both felt when preparing for his expected arrest: 'At which time we sold off all our goods, preparing for a gaol, or banishment where he was desirous I should attend him'.[8] Taken together, Fanshawe and Alleine's narratives suggest that the biographical project in the period was inextricably intertwined with the autobiographical urge, and that, for women, these two generic forms could not easily be divided.

Despite the fact the diary and memoir forms appeared distinguished by their differences, both types of self-representation were closely related. Just as forcefully as the memoir, for instance, the diary could be utilized to reflect more generally on a life experience. Support for this hypothesis comes from the early seventeenth-century diary of Northamptonshire gentlewoman, Lady Grace Mildmay. Nominally a diary, her first-person reflections also encompass an extended account of her childhood, suggesting the mutually constitutive nature of making an entry in a diary and embarking on a longer autobiographical venture. Memoirs, moreover, could be based on, or include extracts from, diaries; alternatively, as this chapter's case study argues, both species of writerly activity may have been linked in a more interwoven and dialectical fashion. To such an alternation between maintaining a daily record and plotting a broader life journey important class dimensions are attached. In the main, only aristocratic women or women from the gentry were permitted the leisure time to write a diary or a memoir, as the names already referred to will have indicated. This is in sharp contrast to women of the middling sort, who participated in radical religious movements and who seem to have exhibited more straightforward autobiographical tendencies. As previous and subsequent chapters show, the priority for the middle-class woman writer was to commit her life to print as part of a testimony of conversion or as a demonstration of prophetic practice. No such imperatives marked the diary and the memoir which, in terms of function, occupied an almost antithetical location and revealed a more socially exclusive provenance.

But this is not to suggest that, because women could be traced to the same class, they necessarily shared identical preoccupations. Politically, diarists and memoirists appear at many removes from each other, a fact which is graphically illustrated when women chronicle local or national happenings and the effect of vicissitudes in the state on their lives. One of the consequences of the Civil War, hardly surprisingly, was to highlight and even exacerbate already existing differences and tensions. For many women, political persuasion was a matter of participation and intervention as well as mental outlook. Central here is Lucy Hutchinson, who, c. 1665, recorded her earlier desperate flight to London to plead for the life of her parliamentarian husband (Colonel John Hutchinson was one of the seven who signed the death warrant of Charles I).[9] In contrast is Anne, Lady Halkett, the active Royalist sympathizer, who makes her key role clear when describing, in 1677–8, how she assisted the Duke of York to escape from London in 1648 by disguising him as a washer-woman.[10] Other women position themselves not so much in relation to a single political perspective but in terms of a more diffuse spectrum of political possibilities available in the period. No one female diarist or memoirist is identical to another, and gravitation to the same genre did not entail the espousal of a unitary political ideology.

Despite their potential for reconstructing the minutiae of some women's lives, diaries and memoirs have tended to be critically neglected, with much of the little work that has been conducted taking the form of 'background' descriptions and summaries. But more nuanced approaches are now being pursued. Recent assessments acknowledge that, although diaries and memoirs offer a peculiarly detailed route into the private domestic space, this does not mean that entry is unmediated. Crucially, these literary forms cannot offer any easy access to a 'true self'. As Edward Said argues, 'in any instance of a written language, there is no such thing as delivered presence, but a re-presence, or a representation'.[11] In other words, following on from Said, no clear-cut relationship between the writer and the 'I' in the text can be posited. Such a realization has particular implications for a study of the diary and the memoir, and the critic approaching these types of writing needs to be forewarned to expect silences and repressions as well as fictional constructions and delusions. Because they allow their readers no straightforward purchase, the contradictory and mutually destabilizing texts of Mary Rich provide an ideal test-case for an investigation into a seventeenth-century woman's autobiographical endeavour.

CASE STUDY: MARY RICH, COUNTESS OF WARWICK, *DIARY* (1666–78) AND *MEMOIR* (*c.* 1671)

An intensely productive writer, Mary Rich (née Boyle), Countess of Warwick, penned hundreds of pages of prayers and meditations in addition to a voluminous diary and a shorter memoir.[12] Each of these texts is distinct in form. The diary, which begins on 25 July 1666 and concludes in April 1678, eighteen months before Rich's death, is composed of almost daily entries of varying length. Dating from around 1671, the memoir is a more structured narrative, which recounts an entire personal history from birth to old age. Despite such obvious differences, both narratives address Rich's marriage, her relationships with family and friends, and her spiritual beliefs. Both are ostensibly private, although traces of revision, a refusal to detail particularly sensitive issues and signs of self-censorship may suggest that, at some level, a reader was borne in mind. Any sense of separation between the texts is

74

additionally blurred since, certainly on one occasion, Rich was writing them both simultaneously.

This fact makes the slippery and elusive character of Rich's writing particularly intriguing. While her texts concern themselves with many of the same life experiences, they forcefully disagree on the particular inflections that these experiences attract. In the memoir, Rich's husband, Charles, is presented as a gallant and romantic hero; in contrast, in the diary, he appears as a violent and abusive tyrant. The diary relationship between Rich and her husband has conflict, disharmony and mental abuse as its signature, in sharp contradistinction to the life story, where the relationship is discovered as a loving ideal. In the life story and the diary, then, are two very different self-presentations, two different lives, which are diametrically opposed and united only in their essential experiential contours.

At once in the memoir it is Rich's indebtedness to romantic motifs and structures that impresses. The memoir's thematic and episodic emphasis – such as the need to privilege true love over parental wishes, and the drive to secure marriage in the face of untold adversity – mimics the preoccupations of popular romances and theatre productions. Correspondences between individual characterizations and contemporary romantic stereotypes are rife. For example, Rich constructs herself as the typical romantic heroine: beautiful, wealthy, resolutely moral, eminently eligible and in considerable demand (A. 3). A dovetailing between Rich and the romantic heroine is never more evident than when she expresses her dissatisfaction with the prospect of an arranged marriage. Faced with 'many great and advantageous offers', she cannot 'endure to hear of any of them' (A. 4). True to the spirit of the high-minded aristocratic protagonist, Rich turns her back on convention to find her own destiny, even as her narrative simultaneously reveals its implication in a panoply of romantic ideologies.

Several contemporary statements establish that Rich was cognizant of romance genres. Moreover, one of the points of contact between the diary and the memoir is a repeated suggestion that the author spent the years 1639 to 1650 'in nothing else but reading romances and seeing plays' (A. 8).

Lending support to Jacqueline Pearson's arguments about the familiar place of recreational reading in a contemporary woman's life, these allusive traces of literate activity show that Rich was both a consumer of the French heroic romances so popular in England in the mid seventeenth century and a theatre-goer responsive to dramatic romances and romantic elements circulating in plays in a pre-Civil War theatrical culture.[13]

At the same time, these references point up the fact that recreational reading in a contemporary woman's life history invariably occupied a fractured site. In Rich's case, reading romances seems to have generated conflicting emotions: pleasure and guilt intermingle in overlapping ways. Implicit, too, in Rich's repeated spotlighting of her cultural and literary activities is a retrospective recognition of a text's shaping power and determining effects. At such moments, Rich constructs romance as a generic phenomenon which played a persuasive role in her life trajectory. The force of her insight into the influence of genre is reflected in the memoir's structure. Easily translatable into an unmediated romantic form, it is the inception of Rich's relationship with Charles which is privileged, and, strikingly, in a text which presents itself as the definitive narrative of a whole life, nearly three-quarters of its space is devoted to an elaboration of the courtship period.

If a structural reading suggests a thorough internalization of the conventions of romance, however, an assessment of Rich's memoir in juxtaposition with her diary plays arresting variations on the theme. The author's writings may invest in romance, but this is not to suggest that Rich consumed its fictions uncritically. Indeed, the diary forcefully articulates the discrepancy between the idealization of the heterosexual union in romance and the 'reality' of married life. Most immediately, perhaps, there is an implicit criticism of romantic aspirations in the discovery of the love-match's 'actuality', with the diary electing not to pursue the romantic narrative option. Instead, the diary focuses upon numerous instances of marital disharmony, pointing up the potentially transient nature of sentimental attachment. References to violent and prolonged 'disputes' between husband and wife punctuate the entries, while registrations of Charles' outbursts of rage are a staple of the diary's construction. Moreover, because Rich uses a similar terminology when she articulates moments of marital crisis, her narrative takes on some of the properties of a balladic refrain:

> After dinner, without any occasion given, my lord fell into great passion with me . . . He fell violently passionate against me . . . My lord was passionate with me without any occasion . . . My lord, without any occasion given by me, fell into a great passion with me. (*M.* 74, 103, 131, 136)

Whether she is using the expression conventionally ('without any occasion given, my lord fell into great passion with me') or inverting it with an almost desperate persistence ('was passionate with me without any occasion'), the effect is to suggest that strife, for the author, has become a matter of routine. Phrases delineating her resultant unhappiness reverberate throughout the diary, to the extent that it is possible to trace a pattern of entries linking despair and domestic conflict. At least as the diary expresses it, Rich's relationship with Charles is clearly a source of romantic disillusionment.

More explicitly, criticism is manifested in the diary's trenchant attack on romance's delusive qualities and coercive power. At those moments in the diary when Rich meditates upon the theme of unrealized expectations and broken dreams, her construction in the autobiography of Charles as 'the source of all her happiness' (*A.* 9) attracts particularly ironic inflections. United in the similarity of their phrasing and wording, the common preoccupation of such moments is the divide between expectations and outcomes, the gap that separates Rich's hoped-for life and its material embodiment. The disparity is encapsulated most powerfully in diary statements which find their *raison d'être* in trenchantly turned antithetical conjunctions; as Rich writes, her 'bitterest crosses come from that creature that I did expect my sweetest comforts from' (*M.* 219). Through its alignment of oppositional possibilities, Rich's text draws a heightened attention to her life's disappointments although, interestingly, without placing blame upon 'that creature', Charles. Instead, her ill-founded affection and poor choice of marriage partner are displaced onto her own romantic longings (and hence, I would suggest, onto the desires and emotions created by her reading of romance). The author broods, for instance, on 'the great dissatisfactoriness I had found in [the] things that I had set my heart upon and expected happiness from' (M. 219), illuminating a profound disjunction between what she has been encouraged to believe by an insidious cultural mythology and what hard experience has taught her to confront. In such formulations, Rich comes close to the realization that romantic love has been less an ideal for her sense of well-being than a chimera that has cost her personal contentment.

The full implications of this self-knowledge only appear when one compares Rich's use, in the memoir, of romantic love as an explanation for filial estrangement with the diary's particular tone of regret. Frequent reference is made in the diary to the 'undutiful and disobedient' (M. 123) way in which Rich had forced her father to consent to her marriage. The unhappy marriage is read by Rich as her punishment for refusing filial subservience. Out of her resistance to the patriarch, Rich believes, the troubles of her own union were born; as she states: 'The sin that in an especial manner God was pleased to break my heart for was my disobedience to my father; this sin I did bemoan with plenty of tears, and confessed God was righteous in letting me read my sin in my punishment' (M. 247). One kind of disobedience (to the father) here blurs with another (to the deity), as Rich castigates herself for a transgression that has made her not so much a romantic heroine as a familial outcast.

In the memoir, narrative strategy works in a complementary fashion to link romance and the experience of daughterly rejection. Passages of of intense vacillation illuminate the battle between 'duty' and 'passion' (A. 4), situating as polarities the will of the father and the requirements of the romance genre. An implicit opposition simultaneously emerges between the sublimity of Rich's feelings and her father's financially inflected sensibility (opposition to the match is viewed by Rich as an antipathy towards Charles' unimpressive economic credentials): 'when I married my husband, I had nothing of . . . fortune in my thoughts; it was his person I . . . cared for, not an estate' (A. 10), the author states. More broadly, the memoir exteriorizes personal and familial entanglement in such a way as to absolve Rich herself from romantic responsibility. Charles, for example, is represented as someone who 'did insensibly steal away my heart and got a greater possession of it than I knew he had' (A. 4), the deflective power of words such as 'possession' and 'steal' pointing to a heroine in a situation beyond her control. This is reinforced by the way in which the relationship between Mary and Charles is made to develop via a series of chance happenings and fortuitous interventions, emphasizing a romantic conception of destiny and fate. All culminates in a climactic statement that figures love as the key instrument with which Rich dares her father's anger and overcomes her own fear of disobedience: 'the extraordinarily great kindness I had for Mr Rich made me resolve to endure anything for his sake' (A. 6). Given the legitimating morality with which romance is invested at this point, one can assume that, for Rich, the genre proved abundantly enabling and sustaining.

Comfort and self-justification may inhere, too, in the alternative subject positions that Rich entertains in the diary. Like one of the saints, whose torments were described in works such as John Foxe's sixteenth-century *Book of Martyrs*, or like the pious Mrs Smith, the contemporary heroine of one of the exemplary biographies she reads, Rich commemorates a sense of suffering in terms of the hagiography that occupied so crucial a place in seventeenth-century culture, seeing herself as cast in an almost sacrificial mould. The following extracts offer an indication of these self-flattering, strategic reinventions:

> After dinner, my lord fell into an exceeding violent passion with me . . . I was in no fault to provoke him to it, and, blessed be God, I was enabled to bear his passion without saying anything to provoke him to continue it. (M. 154)

> He fell in a much more passionate manner upon me . . . and vented against me more passionate words than ever I heard him (whore) . . . I was by God's goodness to me kept from answering one word . . . and was enabled to go on . . . doing my duty . . . returning good for evil . . . if ye do well and suffer for it and take it patiently, this is acceptable to God.[14]

In these two separate entries, the first date dated 1668 and the second 1673, one can trace a trajectory leading from an initially resigned acceptance of domestic abuse to a more divinely sanctioned and actively engaged argument for a state of prevalent distress. The second quotation, in particular, plays up Rich's self-appointed role as an embodiment of patient forbearance. A Christ-like figure whose tribulations can be traced to her husband's misdeeds, Rich constructs herself as a singular example of the trials of virtue.

The ease with which Rich is able to assemble a martyrology is related to the fact that discourses of self-sacrifice offer not only a validation but also a rationale for domestic and marital friction. Rich's investment in a scripturally inspired interpretation of her fraught personal circumstances plays itself out in the ways in which frequent broodings on troubled circumstances are balanced by formulaic observations. After tolerating Charles' rages, she is prone to state: 'It was for my profit and good . . . I was enabled to justify God's proceedings with me, and to say, it was good for me that I was afflicted' (M. 190). Since, in the martyrological tradition, affliction is a prerequisite for salvation, reflections on heaven in the diary, unsurprisingly, inspire a train of escapist fantasies: death is constructed both as a deliverance from and as a reward for daily troubles. Hence, after an evening spent listening to the vulgar conversation of her husband and his brother, Rich consoles herself with the thought that:

> When I came to heaven I should never more have my soul grieved at the hearing of the filthy communication of the wicked, but instead . . . hear the hallelujahs of the blessed . . . one moment in heaven would make me forget all the crosses of this life. (M. 191)

Seeing herself through the lens of another crucifixion, and consoling herself with the conviction that her tribulations will pave the way to eternal happiness, Rich seems to find a healthy measure of satisfaction in the conviction that her husband is an unlikely candidate for heavenly glory.

At one and the same time, however, the diary contains evidence to suggest that Rich utilized discourses of exemplary biography to interrogate the roles (wife and mother) that contemporary morality required her to serve. An intriguing feature of her narrative is the extent to which Rich almost always parallels her care for her husband with her forced neglect of godly duties. Comments on the obligation to attend her husband's sickbed are frequently followed (usually in the same sentence) by references to having to miss divine worship; as she states: 'In the afternoon, my lord had a fit of an ague, *and so I was kept from being retired* by my attendance upon him' (*M.* 77; my italics). The tension in the extract arises from the way in which Charles and God are situated in vexed and explicit opposition. Just as Charles is envisaged as a barrier to Rich's godly or 'quality' time, so are domestic matters seen as intervening in her need for personal communion. In their deployment of a language of compulsion and burdensome necessity, the following extracts highlight such a negative construction of household responsibilities:

> having heard of some disorder among some of my servants, I was forced to spend most of the morning in . . . counselling them . . . In the afternoon, I was *hindered, by necessary employments*, from being retired. (*M.* 199, 76; my italics)

Once again, the syntactical arrangement of the prose points to the other, more attractive (but threatened) location of Rich's inner space. Because Rich describes husband and household in an identically idiomatic manner, moreover, she bestows upon both a similarly levelling gaze. Interestingly, an absorption in antithesis is absent from Rich's descriptions of time spent with female friends and relatives; instead, here we find a sentence structure characterized by a free-flowing and accumulative narrative style.

Extending the suggestion that God and Charles are generally opposed is the idea that they are locked in a specific rivalry for Rich's affections. On 11 April 1668, she notes: 'I had a sweet enjoyment of God this happy morning, for some two hours together whilst my lord slept' (*M.* 152). Clearly peeping through the entry is the notion of a clandestine, adulterous relationship, and this is more forcefully elaborated in passages in which Rich mourns the the extinction of romantic love: 'God is . . . so merciful . . . as to throw down our idol and his rival, and to make it . . . seem withered in our eyes by having a less blinded passion for that person' (*M.* 262). Romantic love, from the evidence of Rich's scriptural appropriations and applications of her reading to her own life, is equivalent to a form of idolatry. And, while the displacement of earthly love onto a heavenly object was strongly encouraged in the devotional literature of the period, with many women describing their relationship to God in a highly stylized romantic vocabulary, the extraordinary ardour and sexual charge characterizing Rich's practice of religious exercises in the diary suggest that an erotic transference between Charles and God takes place:

> It pleased God . . . in a more than ordinary manner to draw out the strength of my affections; and . . . to find my heart inflamed with love to him . . . with desire I did desire him, and found I esteemed him before the whole world.   (M. 84–5, 185)

In earlier diary passages, religious and romantic languages collided. Now, however, they exist in a mutually constitutive accord, which suggests that spiritual longings and romantic imperatives find their meeting-place in the personal relationship between a male divinity and a female believer. With this final mobilization of a contemporary genre, then, romance is subsumed inside a broader discourse of predestination: the difficult relationship with Charles becomes the way to God, the route to earthly escape.

The concluding stages of the memoir offer corroboration for such a hypothesis. Throughout, Rich's narrative has suggested the existence of a benevolent influence. However, it is only as the courtship concludes that this influence is interpreted less as the inexorable working out of romance than as the force of God moving in his mysterious ways. Romance, in short, is constructed not only as the guarantor of happiness but as the medium through which Rich is able to secure a *rapprochement* with the divine: 'I by my marriage thought of nothing but having a person for whom I had a great passion . . . yet [God] was pleased . . . to bring me, *by my marriage*, into a . . . religious family' (*A*. 15; my italics). The manoeuvre staged here has a particularly paradoxical flavour. For even as Rich is conceptualizing marriage as the perfect embodiment of romantic love, she suggests that her blessed union is part of a grander scheme culminating in a relationship with another master.

The textual deployments of Mary Rich demonstrate the extent to which a woman can appropriate even the most coercive of narratives, putting stories and formulas to politic use. None of these processes, moreover, rules out the other: across Rich's *oeuvre*, her strategies change across time, alerting us to the fact that the creation of an individual subjectivity is never static, that it is frequently coterminous and that several different (and even contradictory) interpretive responses can crystallize at one and the same time. Rich's inscription of multiple and competing personalities undermines the illusion that her identity may be contained within either the frame of exemplary biography or the confines of romantic femininity, although, of course, it is through both of them that she chooses expediently to speak. While Rich is deeply implicated in both discourses, neither of them contains her adequately or wholly. The diary and the autobiography together offer up a Rich stamped with a necessarily hybridized nature and reveal a woman governed by, and born out of, the material contradictions which informed any seventeenth-century female sense of self.

6

Conversion Narratives

GENRE, RANGE, WRITERS

This chapter looks at a form of writing in which many women participated but which has hitherto received virtually no critical attention. Conversion narratives are testimonies of personal religious development related by members of seventeenth-century Puritan churches; as first-person accounts, they commemorate either a complete life history or a substantial part of a life history. Central to the narrative's trajectory is the focus upon a pivotal episode – an experience of enlightenment that 'proved' to the author and to others the authenticity of the convert's heavenly credentials. Unlike diaries or memoirs, then, conversion narratives are not simply records of personal experience. Instead, they might be seen as highly structured searches for divine approbation, as codified registrations of an individual journey to godliness.

The impulse behind the conversion narrative enterprise derives from Puritan theological teaching about entrance to the faith. Crucially, lying behind a narrative's attempts to demonstrate the destiny of its author is a spiritual belief in predestination (the Calvinist philosophy which assigned a subject either damnation or salvation according to divine design) and election (the notion that only a select few will enjoy eternal life). Accordingly, a will to self-examination becomes one of the conversion narrative's most salient signatures and is reflected in the genre's textually introspective focus. Typical, in this connection, is the narrative *Satan His Methods and Malice Baffled* (1683) by Hannah Allen, which has been selected as this chapter's case study. Notably, Allen writes 'to see what God will do with me', simultaneously expressing a belief in an omnipotent deity and constructing her life as a script in which individual elective standing and spiritual destiny might easily be discerned.[1]

Thousands of narratives of this kind were written between 1640 and the turn of the century, and a substantial proportion of them (almost 100) had women as their authors. Extant texts can be usefully split into two groups. The first is oral in origin. That is, the narrative's first incarnation was as a spoken testimony delivered to the congregation of a church (usually, although not exclusively, Baptist or Independent) to which the speaker was hoping to gain membership. In these cases, the text functioned as evidence of the applicant's sterling qualities and, hence, worthiness to win admission. On many occasions, oral conversion narratives of such a kind found their way into print by being collected and published by the church's minister; no less than sixty-one relations, for instance, many the work of women, appear in *Spiritual Experiences of Sundry Believers* (1653), the record of Henry Walker's Independent congregation at Martin Vintry in London. Accounts of conversion in these compilations tend to be relatively brief and range from only a few pages to up to thirty pages. But others take on a greater level of detail and are more substantial in terms of volume. In this category, narratives were published either as a part of a theological text (as in the case of Elizabeth Moore's *Evidence for Heaven*, 1657, which appears in a section of Edmund Calamy's argument against separation from the national church) or, more usually, as separate works in their own right (as in the case of Sarah Davy's *Heaven Realized*, 1670, which runs to more than 150 pages).[2]

Both oral narratives and their longer counterparts share distinguishing hallmarks which would have been intimately familiar to contemporary godly readers. By the second half of the seventeenth century, the conversion narrative had established its own set of conventions. The expected structure was one of false belief in the writer's salvation, followed by a period of (often agonizing) doubt and then renewed confidence. The outcome of the narrative, therefore, is never open to question. Like the modern consumer of detective fiction or romance, the reader of Allen, Davy and Moore's conversion narratives is already cognizant of the essential sequence and can expect an inexorable movement through a foreordained pattern towards a satisfying closure. Nor was a conventional structural arrangement the only formulaic element deployed. The seventeenth-century reader might reasonably anticipate certain moral dilemmas to be raised and resolved en route: the most popular of these include the author's coming to understand that she can play no part in ensuring her own salvation, and learning to recognize that passive abandonment to God is the only way forward. Predictable episodes abound, since the typical author relates the pricking of conscience upon hearing a particular sermon, the violent tussles with despair which ensue, a refusal to listen to a relative's words of comfort and, most dramatically, a mid-narrative suicide attempt. Such narrative meanderings are usually rounded off with a formal statement of numbered 'evidences' of faith and/or an enumeration of exemplary biblical passages. The conventions of the form, in short, largely predetermine the narrative's shape. Indeed, such is the shaping power of the general design that a dovetailing of experiences among congregation companions was often cited as in itself a sure indicator of the soul bound for glory.

No doubt in part because of their utilization of ready-made frameworks, established trials and conventional linguistic formulations, conversion narrative models proved attractive to those members of the community, such as women, who were either uneducated or unpractised in the writing art. Despite women occupying prominent roles in the form, however, extant texts point to an acute sensitivity on the parts of the authors to their gendered status. Nearly all female-authored conversion narratives are anxious to disclaim a desire for publication, and both Allen and Davy are characteristic in that they elaborate a representative of traditional authority (in Allen's case, her minister, in Davy's case, her husband) as the agency behind the print process. Of course, many aspects of the narratives suggest that their authors' protests are probably closer to the traditional 'modesty topos' than genuine angst, with most accounts exhibiting every sign of being written with audiences or readers in mind: Allen, for example, seems urgently concerned to facilitate the reader's comprehension, often interrupting her prose with explanatory remarks in parentheses. Ultimately, therefore, configurations of reluctance over the publishing question function to foster a sense of womanly decorum, to highlight the author's exemplary nature and to recommend her writing to an interested public.

In keeping with the public potential of their work, most conversion narrative authors invest in the assertion of textual utility. Both Davy and Allen explicitly express a will to be found spiritually useful, thereby granting to their writing a sense of purpose. Having discovered reading to have been helpful to her own growth, Davy hopes that the record of her experience 'might be profitable to some precious soul'.[3] By the same token, Allen imagines others undergoing comparable trials to herself and, possibly, turning to her narrative for guidance. Such a projected interpretation of her record provides justification for her 'desire . . . that . . . this [her experiences] . . . may be known' (S. 72). This quotation focuses interest on the cultural work that the texts will be made to perform and on the contemporary mindset that others are invited to imitate. Lending support to the texts' construction of a practical application is an accompanying system of male editing, authorizing, exhorting and interpreting that, surrounding female-authored conversion narratives, is unprecedented in the period in its weight and scope. An anonymous male editor leads the way through Allen's *Satan His Malice Baffled*, while Jane Turner's *Choice Experiences*, a conversion narrative published in 1653, is printed with a prefatory apparatus made up of recommendations to the reader by her husband, her minister and a third (unnamed) male interpreter. It was not enough, it seems, for the female convert to speak unaccompanied; her work also required the backing and packaging of masculine approval. Paradoxically, the inclusion of prefatory material represented a gesture that was both potentially censorious (since the life is on display, the editor's role is to prevent possible criticism being levelled at the author for going against contemporary notions of female modesty and retirement) and purposefully celebratory. Hence, the editor of Davy's *Heaven Realized* is of the hope that 'younger persons (especially young gentlewomen) will be greatly affected with this precious example':[4] like the author herself, the editor agitates to incorporate her story within a broader, didactic imperative. Similarly, Turner's editor sees in her 'a glorious example for all Christians to follow . . . being so seasonable for the time we live in'.[5] With all female-authored conversion narratives, a process of exemplary construction works to project the converts' highlighted qualities onto other women, thus elaborating the authors as models of proper behaviour. (For instance, Turner's editors describe a woman 'naturally given to the exercise of godliness', 'excelling in grace', 'sweet', 'cautious', 'humble', 'watchful', 'patient', 'forgiving', 'suffering', 'forbearing' and 'virtuous'.[6]) As the authors of conversion narratives had structured themselves around the dictums of the Puritan preachers, then, so do they emerge as models to be mobilized in the religious community at large.

Interestingly, this seventeenth-century sense of its imitative utility has continued into modern assessments of the conversion narrative's value as a literary form. In recent criticism, conversion narratives have tended to be judged in terms of an undifferentiated corpus as opposed to a body of work consisting of discrete interventions. Effectively, because of their adherence to formula, conversion narratives have been prevented from being considered as imaginative expression in their own right. However, more recently, other critics have begun to suggest that, while a formula is certainly operative in the conversion text, it does not constitute the whole story. In a move which firmly posits them as objects worthy of individual study, the conversion narratives of Allen, Davy and Joan Vokins are excerpted in the anthology *Her Own Life: Autobiographical Writings by Seventeenth-Century Englishwomen*, the editors claiming that 'even when the experiences recorded are similar to those of other Nonconformist confessors . . . there is an individual voice here, speaking of herself'.[7] The argument that an authentically speaking subject can be attended to even within the most hidebound of conventional strictures has important links with recent work in the field of cultural studies. Even as they recognize that a large percentage of books, magazines, films and television drama depend on formulaic arrangements, cultural critics have argued that each conventional utterance has a wide-ranging interpretive potential and, as such, should not be relegated to an inferior status.

Instead, critics hold that a clear conception of the sets of conventions authors choose to observe is crucial to effective evaluation: it is from the interplay between the formula and the producer's own personal concerns that artistry arises.

This newer critical consensus contains the possibility for opening up the conversion narrative to more nuanced readings. Immediately, in conversion narratives authored by women, it can be seen that the interaction between 'convention' and 'invention' is noticeably gendered. Customarily, the conversion narrative levels representational credentials; because the formula places the most profound significance on the retrospective interpretation of experience, rather than the experience itself, any experience, in theory, is as significant as the next. The effect is to permit events commonly regarded as key stages in female existence – courtship, marriage and childbirth – to be validated as appropriate subjects for study. Events chosen for representation by Davy and Allen certainly demonstrate a reliance upon everyday occurrences not always regarded through a 'literary' lens. Davy, for example, chooses to describe her childhood, the deaths of her younger brother and mother, a long-standing illness, years of isolation, a meeting with a woman who was to be a great influence, and marriage quite late in life. In the same way, Allen recounts a religious upbringing, a faith-inspiring book, marriage, admission to Edmund Calamy's church, the birth of her only child, the subsequent death of her husband, a period of dependent widowhood, a depressive illness and eventual remarriage.

To contextualize the mutually enabling dialectic between quotidian experience and a representation of female concerns, it might be helpful to speculate about those contemporary forces allowing the formula to be put into play. We know that one of the conventional imperatives of the conversion formula is to reanimate moments of self-doubt, pain and despair; it might not be unreasonable to assume, then, that, during the selection process, the writer recalls and narrates those times in her life which have affected her most. It might also be possible to infer that the periods granted prominence are those which, from the perspective of the writing act, seem to have been particularly traumatic and psychically disruptive. In this regard, in the peculiar preoccupations of female-authored narratives may lie a key to the animating anxieties that fashioned women at this historical juncture. Certainly, it is worth noting that, apart from the expected concentration on matters relating to churches and theology, what stands out in these autobiographical highlights is an investment in family, in relationships with parents, siblings, husbands and children, and in the various stages – childhood, marriage and widow-hood – whereby female existence was constituted. Indeed, in the often exhaustive analyses of the feelings clustering around these very 'feminine' subject areas, it is tempting to posit the authors' gendered identities as the bedrock from which springs initial despair and subsequent tribulation.

The case study focuses on those moments which individual-ize one narrative, arguing that the conversion narrative for-mula affords ample glimpses of a female subjectivity striving for authentic articulation. It is suggested that, via distinctive narrative peculiarities (the elaboration of spaces hovering uncertainly between 'convention' and 'invention'), Hannah Allen's *Satan* reveals itself as exceeding 'official' interpretations and opening up new representational options.

CASE STUDY: HANNAH ALLEN, *SATAN HIS METHODS AND MALICE BAFFLED* (1683)

The title page of Allen's conversion narrative provides us with two possible 'keys' to interpreting her experience. At once, the full title of the book ('A Narrative of God's Gracious Dealings with . . . Mrs Hannah Allen . . . Reciting the Great Advantages the Devil Made of Her Deep Melancholy, and the Triumphant Victories . . . God Gave Her over All His Stratagems') directs the reader to the expected interpretation of the narrative: Allen's troubled history is understood as the tale of her overcoming, through God's intervention, Satan's temptations to despair and suicide. As the end of Allen's conversion makes clear, essential to maintaining this particular interpretive framework is the narrative's utilization of the retrospective form. The final words take the action into the present day, placing responsibility of understanding in the mouth of Allen herself. If her experiences were 'a bitter cup', she argues, then this was because they touched so keenly on 'what the only wise God saw I had need of' (*S.* 73). Constantly emphasized through the narrator's use of the past tense, through periodic passages of summary, through reflective commentaries and through calling up, in the text, materials written at a much earlier date, the retrospective form works to reinforce the 'official' interpretation, reminding readers not only that the events recounted have taken place some time earlier, but also that the autobiography is composed from a place of spiritual calm and divine proximity. Within the framework set up by the narrative, the closing biblical passsages, including the following (James 5:11), make a special sense: 'Behold we count them happy which endure; ye have heard of the patience of Job, and have seen the end of the Lord; that the Lord is very pitiful and of tender mercy' (*S.* 79). To bear suffering, in the same way as the author, is to be rewarded with eternal joys, even to join those other fellow notables of the biblical pantheon. Allen's text, then, is neatly framed within a conservative understanding of experience, its meanings grist only for a particular ideological mill.

But such a reading does not answer to the total effect of Allen's text, for, at the same time, the title page offers a second 'key' to interpretation. The opening positions the narrative as a hiatus, as a particular juncture in Allen's life marked by the absence of both a prior and a subsequent spouse: the author is described as 'that Choice Christian ... Afterwards Married to Mr Hatt', while the first line of the text proper situates Allen as 'the Late Wife of Hannibal Allen, Merchant' (*S.* 1). The inclusion of a number of brief passages reflecting on childhood and married life notwithstanding, the space opened up between the two descriptions suggests the narrative as an interregnum, an anomalous interval between husbands. Such an emphasis is appropriate, since the balance between structure and individuation in Allen's narrative ultimately operates to identify as centrally important her widowed status. In particular, via juxtapositions, narrative stresses and the linking of emotion with particular events, the conversion formula allows Allen to articulate feelings of grief at her husband's death and, more importantly, to present a vital construction of the stigma attached to a dependent single woman in seventeenth-century England. In this way, it might be suggested that reading against the account's 'official' interpretation system allows the author to resist the forward pressure of the narrative. The actual contents of the conversion narrative thereby appear not so much as clearly defined stages on a road to recovery but, rather, as the unpredictable confusion of genuine trauma.

As Elspeth Graham has noted, *Satan*'s references to emotional sufferings are always 'established in conjunction with the spiritual'.[8] Hence, Allen's first reference to the medical condition of 'melancholy' is connected directly both with a spiritual effect (the devil is able to tempt a weakened Allen) and a tangible cause (her husband's absence):

> In the time of [my husband's] life, I was frequently exercised with variety of temptations, wherein the devil had the more advantage, I being much inclined to melancholy, occasioned by the oft absence of my dear and affectionate husband, with whom I lived, present and absent, about eight years. (*S.* 6–7)

At this stage, Allen's symptoms remain only mildly depressive: she is characterized by 'an inclination to melancholy' (*S.* 7). It is the death of Mr Allen that triggers a rapid descent into the conversion narrative's familiar period of chronic doubt, which itself is marked by a fear that the author is irrevocably damned, has committed unforgivable crimes and must stand arraigned of hypocrisy:

> After I heard of the death of my husband . . . I began to fall into deep melancholy, and no sooner did this black humour begin to darken my soul, but the devil set on with his former temptations . . . with great strugglings and fightings within me. (*S.* 8)

Diffusing her text almost to the last page is Allen's expression of the anguish following the husband's demise. Formulations such as 'what a dismal dark condition I am in . . . as dark as hell itself' (*S.* 60) testify to the extremity of the author's emotional state, while an early sense of weariness is registered through the insertion into the narrative of extracts from pre-conversion prayers. Here a despairing note is explicitly struck: 'I know not what to say; the Lord pity me in every respect and appear for me, in these my great straits both of soul and body; I know not what to do . . . For Christ's sake, pity my case' (*S.* 18–19), Allen states. When linked to the husband's death, these formulaic expressions of despair take on a particular force, since it is possible to detect within them a unique demonstration of female feeling about a spouse's passing.

The notion that Allen uncovers in the conventions of her genre a means of accessing 'authentic' grief is undergirded by a narrative moment of interpretive anomaly. Throughout, Allen's experiences are heavily punctuated with biblical reference, the latter styled as a comment on the former. Although most of these chime harmoniously with 'official' interpretations of the text, one is singularly out of place. Even if the verse is not quoted in its entirety, an observation about 'the ground of her trouble' (*S.* 40) points the reader to Colossians 3:5 and, in particular, to the idea of an excessive earthly love – 'Mortify therefore your members which are upon the earth; fornication, uncleanness, inordinate affection, evil concupiscence and covetousness, which is idolatry'. Connecting present-day unhappiness to past connubial pleasures, the text gestures to the biblical verse to move away from a straightforward location of despair as the first stage of conversion; instead, Allen inserts a sense of sorrow into a more individual, personalized space. Because Allen's grief is tied to her own material and emotional loss, therefore, despair becomes a potential indicator of the virtues of the earlier relationship and the impact of the subsequent bereavement.

Beyond its despairing deployments, *Satan* plumbs deeper tiers of association and implication. In particular, a denser significance – which suggests that the state of mind constructed by Allen results less from the fact of her husband's death than from the position of dependency forced upon her by her widow's status – inheres in the narrative's representation of more extreme emotional outbursts. The inflexibility of her cultural niche is revealed in those parts of the narrative where Allen identifies with a host of marginal constituencies. Identifying with criminals and vagabonds, she brands herself 'a Magor-Missabib, a terror to . . . all my friends . . . a Hell upon earth . . . the monster' (*S.* 40, 59).[9] Encapsulated in this litany of self-lacerations is a narrative embodiment both of the community from which Allen is excluded and of the author's sense of herself as outcast, a cultural renegade who disrupts contemporary social, familial and behavioural expectations. It is within the context of such a stigmatized ostracization, I think, that we can begin to understand the narrative's repeated articulations of loneliness and yearnings for comfort, which differentiate Allen's expressions of despair from those of her contemporaries.

The connections feeding between outcast and widow constructions are worth elaborating. Depending on their relative positions within the fluctuating band of the middling sort, widows were generally perceived in the early modern period either as economically solvent women in search of a younger husband or as dispossessed unfortunates who were obliged to petition to the courts for state pensions.[10] The knowledge that Allen is a member of the middling sort notwithstanding (her first husband and grandfather were both merchants), it is difficult to ascertain precisely where the author resides in the class scale, especially since financial difficulties make no appearance in the text. However, from the geographical peregrinations traced (in a period of just a few years, locational details move her around half a dozen destinations in the Midlands to as many again in London), and from the expansive cast-list of ministers, friends and relatives with whom Allen comes into contact, it is possible to extract a history of enforced migration and downward social mobility, a not unfamiliar fate for homeless and unemployed women in the early modern period.

The notion that the widow can be passed about – that she represents an unwanted property to be exchanged – is taken up in more emotive parts of the narrative. Harping upon extinction, and repeatedly tormenting herself with evocations of a hellish afterlife, Allen frequently portrays her psychological state with an explosiveness that a modern sensibility might characterize as paranoiac. For example, a portion of the account is devoted to recollecting the period during which Allen repeatedly feels her sanity threatened by the lights and sounds of a neighbouring house: 'if I heard the voice of people talk or read in other houses, I would not be persuaded, but that it was devils like men talking of me and mocking' (S. 34).

Arresting is the implication that Allen's retrospective horror stems not only from the transformation of monsters into men but also from the acknowledgement that she herself is designated a monstrous subject of discussion. In this way, the author reveals an anxiety about the male gaze, an economy of the eye which passes a judgement simultaneously pejorative and infernal ('devils'). Allen's language is entirely characteristic here, since the speaker constantly discovers herself as an object being looked at (ministers compete 'to see [her]', S. 64, and friends read 'death in her face', S. 65). Moreover, the attention to Allen's body, which focuses upon motifs of illness and weight loss, dramatically illuminates this corporeal visibility, while several departures from the first-person account reinforce a readerly sense that she is a specular attraction. Via such narrative emphases and digressions, Allen is moved from a position defined solely by bereavement to one suffused with the gendered expectations and assumptions of her cultural environment.

To highlight only the disenfranchised dimension of Allen's trajectory, however, would be to skirt over the conversion narrative's finer interstices. This is because the stress on the gaze is finely balanced in *Satan* by the ways in which Allen's fervour displays a performative component. The theatrical nature of her suicide attempts, distinguished by melodramatic inaugurations and anti-climactic outcomes, points to strategies deployed, consciously or unconsciously, to gain notice. One of her many thwarted attempts to take her own life finds Allen, at her brother's London house, swallowing spiders in the hope that she might 'die in [her] sleep' (S. 32). The description continues:

> in the night, awaking out of my sleep, I thought I felt death upon me (for I had taken a spider when I went to bed) and called to my brother and told him so, who presently arose and went to his friend an apothecary, who came and gave me something to expel it; the next day my uncles and brother ... removed me to Mr Peter Walker's House ... whose wife was my kinswoman. (S. 33)

With its details of the stirred household, the life or death summoning of the apothecary and the family conference, the passage makes a stunning impression. Equally striking is

Allen's ability to provoke the domestic unit into action; she is removed from a thinly populated house (a place she has described as 'lonesome', S. 33) to one with far more opportunities for social intercourse. The unspoken desire for company betrays a narrative, which, in assiduously registering Allen's defiance ('I would not be persuaded . . . All [entreaties] took no place with me', S. 34, 62), constantly posits the existence of a responsive audience. By doing so, the text plots a course of behaviour which works against the Calvinistic insistence that to cultivate 'solitariness' was the widow's main daily duty and ideal defining virtue.[11] It might also be suggested that moments of performative prominence bear directly upon Allen's attempts to resist anonymity, actively to counter the ideal widow stereotype. Certainly, the text's satisfied reports, communicated in direct speech, of Allen's conversational ripostes and put-downs indicate a delight in linguistic wit and turns of phrase. In short, Allen works to engineer a representational dispensation in which she is the personality on whom attention focuses. Her self-construction accords with her insistence on individuation ('My condition is unparalleled', S. 23) and with her later arguments for her narrative's utility.

Interestingly, Allen's final recovery is represented, not through the conventional conversion narrative's mechanisms of spiritual surety and confidence, but via a series of episodes which have social reintegration and acceptance as their theme:

> I passed that winter much better than formerly, and was pretty comfortable and orderly in the family; and the next summer was much after the same manner, but grew still something better; and the next winter likewise still mending, though but slowly, till the spring began, and then I changed much from my retiredness and delighted to walk with friends abroad. (S. 70–71)

Bolstering the pattern of Allen's reassimilation, and firmly locating despair in widowed circumstances, is the way in which melancholy lifts entirely at remarriage. This move is rationalized not only in terms of affection but also pragmatics: 'It pleased God', Allen writes, 'to provide a very suitable match for me, one Mr Charles Hatt, a widower living in Warwickshire, with whom I live very comfortably, both as to my inward and outward man' (S. 71). In this final construction, the struggle of Allen's autobiographical journey to find a niche in existing cultural arrangements is made abundantly clear. Closure is achieved through wedlock rather than spiritual certainty, and is signalled by an accommodation to dominant gender norms and roles. The construction of 'inward and outward' as co-dependent posits the importance of physical well-being to the speaker's security. Following a route whereby Allen both loses and subsequently gains her sense of self, the conversion narrative demonstrates that, at least for this single woman without independent means, eventual health could only be guaranteed through an earthly marriage that betokens an ultimate meeting with godly authority.

7

Prose Fiction

GENRE, RANGE, WRITERS

To track the emergence of prose fiction by women over the course of the seventeenth century is to remind ourselves of some of the essential considerations involved in the female theatrical tradition. That is, female prose fictions during this period had their beginnings in translations of non-English works. They betrayed, at the outset, non-commercial imperatives, only taking on a commercial orientation by the end of the century. In addition, original prose fiction came increasingly to be the norm, while an earlier aristocratic and gentle bias among female authors eventually gave way to more middle-class and bourgeois social identifications. These developments were stimulated by a new attention to the female consciousness (aided, in part, by treatises devoted to the position of women in society), by a predilection for popular rationalism, by the expansion of the reading audience, and by the growth of the print marketplace. They have their inception, too, in changes in literary fashion and an appetite for European romances, *nouvelles* and letter-novels. Behind the English women writers discussed in this chapter lurk a legion of French and Spanish precursors, such as Madeleine de Scudéry and María de Zayas y Sotomayor. The writers addressed here were distinguished by startling and revolutionary transformations to their chosen idioms, but they arguably found an initial prompt for literary innovation in continental traditions and the productions of their non-native counterparts.

An early instance of such indebtedness is demonstrated in the vogue for translation. Perhaps the first example of a prose fiction by a woman is Margaret Tyler's 1578 translation of the Spanish *The Mirror of Princely Deeds and Knighthood*. Clearly, Tyler was not the sole author, having elected to ventriloquize an already established voice; however, she did include an 'Epistle', which defends her right as 'a woman to pen a story' and to 'discourse in learning' and 'arguments'.[1] The note of bravado sounded was taken up by Lady Mary Wroth later in the seventeenth century: already a practitioner of translation, she was distinctive for authoring *Urania*, the first original prose fiction by a woman, and for securing, in 1621, its publication. Mary Ellen Lamb has argued that Wroth's romance 'disperses a multitude of characters over wide expanses . . . Some of them reappear, and their narratives tangle and untangle . . . Some of them are lost . . . forever'.[2] This is a telling assessment of *Urania*'s mobilization of its leading personalities, and what unites the various strands of the fiction is an emphasis upon constancy. In contrast to the male characters, who are marked by jealousy and inconstancy, the female characters, such as Pamphilia, emerge as the proud owners of a sublime steadiness and fidelity. Indeed, Pamphilia incarnates these virtues, as when, at the alabaster palace, 'Constancy vanished . . . metamorphosing . . . into [the queen's] breast'.[3] By governing her emotions according to a constant logic, Pamphilia accrues to herself a steely self-control and empowering authority, joining other women in the romance who either pursue independent paths or strive against injustices (such as arranged marriages). Vital signs of the resistant female are to be found in the figuration of women reading and writing, and in the sonnet sequence that concludes Part One. Here, a female voice addresses a man (or, at least, emotional extremes gendered as male), thereby appropriating and inverting a masculine poetic convention.

Arguably Wroth felt impelled to position women in a range of emancipated and incarcerated locations because writing *Urania* provided opportunities to reflect upon her own life experience. Wroth's anomalous cultural situation, discussed in chapter 1, invites comparison with that of several of her women characters, while William Herbert, to whom she was scandalously allied, is possibly intended as a version of Pamphilia's elusive Amphilanthus (or 'lover of two'). Such autobiographical resonances lend *Urania* a *roman-à-clef* dimension; certainly, contemporaries read into the romance a commentary on court affairs. Lord Edward Denny, for instance, was so convinced that one of the fiction's stories satirized an arranged marriage between his daughter and a royal favourite that he vituperated Wroth in an accusatory invective: 'Hermaphrodite in show, in deed a monster', he wrote, 'leave idle books alone / For wise and worthier women have written none'.[4] At issue in the verse is not only the 'monstrous' spectacle of a woman writing, but also the danger of an interrogation of enshrined political orthodoxies. Although Wroth denied Denny's inference, and wrote a stinging reply in her defence, she was obliged to withdraw published copies of *Urania* from circulation: the first original prose fiction by a seventeenth-century woman had been sacrificed on the altar of its objecting, masculine detractors.

The romantic genres exploited by Wroth established a pattern for later women writers. Among them, Anna Weamys, who published *A Continuation of Sir Philip Sidney's 'Arcadia'* in 1651, might be considered Wroth's closest literary descendant. However, in plotting a genealogy for seventeenth-century women prose fiction writers, the most obvious beneficiary of Wroth's inheritance would seem to be Margaret Cavendish, Duchess of Newcastle. If Wroth had the stigma of a hermaphrodite forced upon her, Cavendish actively represented herself, in Kate Lilly's formulation, as a 'figurative hermaphrodite. Her idiosyncratic dress combined masculine and feminine elements in a parodic masquerade of gender, while her rare and highly theatrical public appearances never failed to draw an audience'.[5] Hermaphroditism inhered, too, in Cavendish's literary endeavours. Her *Nature's Pictures* (1656), for instance, constitutes a refined generic mixture, since it brings together in a hybridized arrangement moral stories, romances, fictions and an autobiography. Of the romantic fictions featured in the collection, two – 'The Contract' and 'Assaulted and Pursued Chastity' – stand out, centring, as they do, upon young and wealthy heroines who reform their libertine lovers. Agency in these stories belongs with the women (in this sense, Cavendish pushes at the boundaries of romantic ideology), and a militaristic application of virtue is a defining female trait. Similarly,

Cavendish's *The Blazing World*, published in 1666 with *Observations Upon Experimental Philosophy*, presents itself as a *mélange* of styles and influences. First, because of the coupling of the prose fiction with an experimental discussion, Cavendish's utopian fantasy of a woman's rise to a platonic monarchy takes on the properties of a contemporary reflection upon the 'new science'. Second, because women are delineated in bodily terms and via modes of spectacle, *The Blazing World* aspires to a type of autobiography; indeed, the work includes references to Cavendish herself, suggesting, once again, that the author was notable for constantly testing the dividing-lines between literary forms and for purposefully complicating where fact ends and fiction begins.

It is tempting to speculate that Cavendish was excited to extend the generic limits of her writing in the light of wider interventions by contemporary women in the fictional field. Crucially, in the mid to late seventeenth century, literary forms were invariably fluid and amorphous, with women writers being central agents in exploiting the cross-fertilizing possibilities that this lack of fixity facilitated. Thus, Mary Frith was able to produce, in 1662, *The Life and Death of Mary Frith*: nominally an autobiography about a bawd and transvestite, the account is simultaneously a fictionalized rogue narrative, to the extent that it becomes difficult to distinguish which sections are by the author and which are the work of her associates. Cast in a comparable mould is the 1663 text by Mary Carleton, *The Case of Mary Carleton*. Just as the various identities in the narrative shift and blur (Carleton is simultaneously a common bigamist and a wronged 'German Princess'), so do its moral positions and its generic allegiances (apparently autobiographical passages consort with framed *nouvelles*). Beyond the immediate (irresolvable) question of the text's authorship, *The Case of Mary Carleton* makes a singular impact in the ways in which it challenges stereotypes of romantic femininity, for the heroine is constructed both as a defenceless lady and as a witty, desiring subject. Above all, her assumption of different roles is matched, and perhaps even enabled, by the flexibility and variety of the prose medium. Even in a single moment *The Case of Mary Carleton* can imitate the attributes of a range of prose styles, idioms, fictions and modes.

Women prose fiction writers of the seventeenth century, then, foraged adventurously in the genres of their day, mixing and matching forms and vocabularies. No less importantly, they stretched the perimeters of fact, combining and separating out 'true' accounts and 'invented' histories in equal measure. The manipulation of these sorts of literary practice Aphra Behn made her own. Turning to fiction when her drama had incurred disapproval, Behn was unique among her peers in that she privileged the role of female narrators, experimented with narrative technique, reflected on her craft and grafted romance plots onto political critique, all without moralization. First published in 1688, *Oroonoko*, which forms the case study for this chapter, reveals these skills and practices to the full. A concern with kingship and nobility, an implicitly Royalist agenda, a self-conscious application of the female narrator, and an attention to colonial questions – these are some of the defining hallmarks of Behn's prose fiction. In particular, Behn in *Oroonoko* is impelled, as Shakespeare before her, to explore the paradoxically liminal and central cultural location, and the split identifications, of the titular character, the royal slave. Throughout her prose fiction career, Behn was interested, as *Oroonoko* demonstrates, in the intersections between gender, power and morality. Thus, in *The Fair Jilt* (1688), the author explores the situation of a young woman who, once declined, deploys sexual trickery to acquire financial and social aggrandizement: the fiction occupies a notably slippery relationship to contemporary values, since Miranda, the heroine, escapes a conventional punishment. Cast in a similarly shifting ideological mould is *The History of the Nun* (1689). Here, once again, an unsettling scenario, that runs counter to prevailing seventeenth-century notions of propriety, is elaborated. For the narrative concentrates upon an upwardly mobile female subject, upon her amoral social and economic trajectory, and upon the revelation, via the murder of two husbands, of her criminal tendencies. Just as Behn was keen to dissolve into each other 'authentic' and fictional representations, so did she appear concerned to experiment with which species of trangression could be accommodated within her chosen literary forms.

Of Behn's fictional explorations of the fine dividing-line between types of morality, *Love Letters Between a Nobleman and*

His Sister, published in three volumes between 1684 and 1687, can arguably lay claim to be the most eloquent statement. Based upon a (made-up) correspondence between Silvia and Philander, *Love Letters* casts a direct glance at a contemporary scandal – the elopement of Lady Henrietta Berkeley with her brother-in-law, Lord Grey of Werke. Helen Hackett notes that 'Werke was a supporter of the rebel Duke of Monmouth, while the Berkeleys were Tories of the opposite camp'.[6] In other words, *Love Letters* is significant not only as a *roman-à-clef* but as a politically resonant report (two-party fraternization is a subtext), a topically urgent discussion and a quasi-incestuous disquisition (familial unorthodoxy is a major motif). Matching the range of categories into which *Love Letters* can be inserted is a comparably flexible narrative method. While the first volume is epistolary in technique, the second and third rely upon a third-person narrator, a female commentator who allows readers to see, in Janet Todd's words, 'the degeneration of the central pair from lovers to intriguers'.[7] This new voice makes alternative interpretations available, sensitizing us, in an essentially anti-romantic spirit, to the gaps, falsities and inconsistencies involved in self-representational activity. Yet the narrator does not constitute a transparently straightforward phenomenon. As a literary construction, she is simultaneously removed and involved, censorious and sympathetic. The result is that it becomes a hazardous enterprise to attempt to determine the fiction's tone, just as (given its degree of unsettlement) it appears a well-nigh impossible task to fix the text's generic identity.

Behn's experiments with the epistolary form, culled from the work of her European predecessors and contemporaries, were to set the seal on the women writers to follow. More importantly, they provided a model not only for later seventeenth-century female advances in fiction but also for the great flowering of eighteenth-century women novelists. Immediate imitators of Behn arguably include both Catherine Trotter and Delarivier Manley: Trotter's *Olinda's Adventures* (1693) placed in the same melting-pot autobiography, self-defence, romance and a coquettish fictional heroine, while Manley's *Letters Written by Mrs Manley* (1696) derived a thrilling *frisson* from combining the voyage motif, sensational *novellas* and 'realistic' reflection. If nothing else, these writers demonstrate that, by the end of the seventeenth century, prose fiction by women had evolved into a recognized pursuit, and that the female-authored 'novel' was rapidly establishing itself as a permanent fixture in the literary landscape.

CASE STUDY: APHRA BEHN, *OROONOKO* (1688)

Aphra Behn's *Oroonoko* draws heavily on late seventeenth-century constructions of race, and its structure and mindset are shaped by contemporary colonial and imperial practices. Presented by a female narrator, the prose fiction is set in Surinam, an English colony in the West Indies, in which the labour required to work the lucrative sugar plantations is imported courtesy of the thriving African slave-trade.

Throughout *Oroonoko*, Surinam is elaborated in terms of difference, otherness and exoticism. It is likened, at least at the level of its denizens and inhabitants, to a type of freakshow, since it represents a place abundantly stocked with singular creatures, prodigious creations and 'little rarities'.[8] A 'beast in the form and fashion of a lion . . . but . . . in miniature', a snake 'some threescore yards in length' and 'a thousand other birds and beasts of wonderful and surprising forms, shapes, and colours' (p. 75) – these are among the unfamiliar occupants of the Surinam location, and they are catalogued in a dazzled encyclopaedic spirit. Such descriptions have numerous counterparts in contemporary travel literature; they also find their rationale in a fascination with the marvellous, which was both produced by, and itself helped to generate, the colonial project. Mark Thornton Burnett has recently discussed displays of 'monstrous' animals in early modern England, observing that 'spectacles involving strange species worked to secure a sense of national superiority', and he goes on to note that demonstrations of racial difference were no less appealing to the contemporary psyche.[9] At least from the late seventeenth century onwards, if not earlier, the non-English *Homo sapiens*, such as the native African and American, was put on show in fairgrounds, markets, coffee houses and 'cabinets of curiosity' to the delight and horror of the public. *Oroonoko* is deeply rooted in such a culture of exhibition. The narrator discovers the indigenous people of Surinam in a comparable manner to the unveiling of its natural habitat: a rapt interest in nudity, face-painting, body-piercing and scarification is clearly dominant.

Within this context of revelatory spectacles, it is arresting that the first reference to Oroonoko, the prose fiction's titular protagonist, establishes him as 'the wonder of all that world' (p. 79). The language deployed, and the emphasis on wonder, point to the rhetoric of the freakshow and carve out a position for Oroonoko as an extraordinary attraction. Throughout, in fact, Behn's prose fiction imagines the African prince as a phenomenon to be viewed and admired. On first being captured, Oroonoko is taken to a plantation; en route, his companions find that, whenever the party rested, 'numbers of people would flock to behold this man' (p. 107). The metaphorical centre of a travelling show, Oroonoko is delineated as discovering over the course of the fiction that he is the prime recipient of a multitude of gazes. Even the narrator is impelled to seek Oroonoko out in order to 'see him', such is her 'curiosity' (p. 80): the detail of her inquisitiveness evokes, once again, the paying customer in the freakshow booth and aligns the female speaker with the common onlooker.

Intriguingly, it is not the fact of Oroonoko's racial difference alone that attracts notice. As the narrator points out, in slave-trading territory, the sight of African features is not unusual. Rather, it is Oroonoko's particular combination of an exotic racial affiliation and a higher class connection that is found astonishing. Oroonoko's superior birth and breeding are elaborated as shining out, even from beneath his paltry dress, differentiating him from other enslaved Africans and earning him the fiction's oxymoronic alternative title: the work is subtitled *The Royal Slave*. Oroonoko, then, is no simple 'wonder' or 'monster', since the social networks in which he participates confute assumptions about his African alterity.

The protagonist is simultaneously figured as fit to be looked at because, in many respects, he appears less as an African than as a 'mixed-race' creation. Contemporaries were fascinated by the progeny of cross-racial unions, particularly in the light of increasing sexual contact between colonial settlers

105

and indigenous peoples. What excited interest above all was either the spectacle of lighter-skinned blacks or the exhibition of the so-called 'white negro', the 'biological oddity' who, in Barbara Maria Stafford's words, revealed splotches and splashes of a 'discordant epidermal' whiteness on an otherwise black background.[10] Clearly, Oroonoko is not the possessor of such 'partial albinism'; however, he is regarded as a bizarre anomaly because he seems black and beautiful at one and the same time. In *Oroonoko*, to be beautiful means a capacity to demonstrate European features. As several critics have noted, Oroonoko incarnates this requirement: his appearance is thoroughly westernized; his black skin is offset by a nose which is 'rising and Roman, instead of African and flat'; and his mouth is 'far from those great turned lips, which are so natural to the rest of the Negroes' (p. 81). Western standards of beauty are clearly in operation here, to the extent that Oroonoko's fantastic strangeness and status as a spectacle can be traced to a hybridized conjunction of African and European physical appearances.

Like Shakespeare's Othello, Oroonoko exploits the uniqueness of his aesthetic constitution through rhetoric. Enlisting European notions of morality, romance and honour, Oroonoko trades upon his exoticism by telling stories which highlight the perceived differences of his cultural origins. His narratives of his early years, some presented directly from his own mouth, others mediated through the narrator's reinscriptions, rehearse the barbaric nature of African warfare, the opulence of the sub-Saharan courts and the licentiousness of their harems, offering a vision that feeds directly into stereotypical seventeenth-century constructions. At times, Oroonoko's verbal disquisitions are accompanied by the display of a visual 'curiosity', as when the bullet-riddled heart of a killer lion 'gave Caesar [Oroonoko] occasion of many fine discourses, of accidents in war, and strange escapes' (p. 119). Once again, Oroonoko is seen as intimately related to a local culture of 'monstrous' exhibition, although here he appears less the 'monster' at the heart of the booth than the impresario who manages its professional exposure. The contrasting modalities of narration in *Oroonoko* (as should now be clear, the fiction espouses the strategies of travel literature, factual accounts and foreign romances) have puzzled critics. But these different telling elements can be explained, at least in part, by attending to their points of origin in various characters' mouths. Elaborated as tales of Oroonoko's own invention, the romance dimensions of the fiction both participate in the protagonist's rarefied construction and underline his attraction for an English audience.

Oroonoko's absorption in the popular romance motifs of the time is typical of the ways in which the westernization of the central character extends into other psychic areas. In terms of attitudes and behaviour, Oroonoko emerges as the ideal Restoration hero, in possession of 'morals, language and science' (p. 80) and even a European education (courtesy of travelling French, English and Spanish merchants and dignitaries). For much of the narrative, Oroonoko's internalization of western standards and behaviours appears absolute. He is represented, for example, as spending hours deploring the beheading of Charles I: the local detail points to an avoidance of the prince's own political models in favour of an English alternative. Similarly, upon marriage, Oroonoko eschews his country's convention of polygamy, choosing, instead, a European system of monogamy. His selection of love object is envisaged as a universal, if not a western, preference. Although precisely portrayed along racialized lines, Imoinda is simultaneously drawn as a woman with whom 'no man, of any nation . . . did not fall in love' (p. 110). The cost of Oroonoko's internalization of practices not his own might be glimpsed in the narrative attention to his hairstyle; as the narrator states: 'His hair came down to his shoulders, by the aids of art; which was, by pulling it out with a quill, and keeping it combed, of which he took particular care' (p. 81). This is, then, not so much a natural African curl as a straightened European coiffure, a visual signature of severed allegiance and a powerful registration of Oroonoko's own construction of values as performance.

But deeper interstices of the narrative suggest that Oroonoko, contrary to the identifications in which he invests, does not entirely contravene the black stereotype. Linking the representation of Oroonoko, the imaging of his countrymen and the depiction of the natives of Surinam is the prose fiction's insistence upon these three groups' shared *naïveté*.

Oroonoko's *naïveté* is explicitly formulated as a general conviction of goodness, which emanates from his entrenched entertainment of honour. Hence, Oroonoko believes the promise of imminent release, despite the fact that the slave-trader who makes the pledge has already shown himself to be utterly untrustworthy: 'Oroonoko, whose honour was such as he never had violated a word in his life himself . . . believed in an instant what this man said' (p. 103). Even when he is again betrayed, Oroonoko will not relinquish his attachment to trust. Although recognizing that 'he had little reason to credit the words of a backearary' (p. 107), he still makes friends with, and places confidence in, the slave-dealing Trefry, only to be ultimately deceived.[11] The prince's guileless comprehension of humanity places him in the company of Surinam's indigenous inhabitants, who, types of Adam and Eve in a paradisial environment, labour in a pre-lapsarian state of innocence. Such an elaboration of non-English understanding, of a consciousness that allows for no acknowledgement of 'vice, or cunning, but when . . . taught by the white men' (p. 77), not only complicates the ennobled figuration of Oroonoko developed elsewhere; it also levels an accusatory finger at the double-sided cultural consequences of the imposition of a white hegemony.

Other sections of the fiction suggest a more firmly rooted connection between Oroonoko and his black compatriots. The scarified faces and amputated anatomies of the Indian village chieftains, which appear 'so frightful a vision . . . so dreadful a spectacle' (p. 123) to the visiting narrator, prefigure the horrible corporeal dissections of Oroonoko's own end. A practice of self-mutilation is, midway through the fiction, deemed 'a sort of courage too brutal to be applauded by our black hero' (p. 124); by the close, however, Oroonoko embraces precisely such a violent inhumanity, suggesting that the distance he has travelled from the local tribesmen is not as great as it initially appears. Similarly, Oroonoko, his countrymen and the colony's slave population prefer suicide to martial defeat, which points to a black solidarity that resists the traditional Christian equation between sin and taking one's own life.

Connections such as these are absorbing, not least because the dominant tendency in criticism of the prose fiction has been to stress Oroonoko's links, not with other racialized figures, but with women and, in particular, the female narrator. Certainly, an alliance is formed between the daughter of the governor and the royal slave, to the extent that Oroonoko is 'scarce an hour in a day from [her] lodgings' (p. 113). The friendship that develops is one in which the gender of the narrator is a central consideration: '[Oroonoko] liked the company of us women much above the men, for he could not drink, and he is but an ill companion in that country that cannot' (p. 113), it is stated. Oroonoko's liking for these women complements, and is of a piece with, his sympathetic treatment of women in general (Behn frequently contrasts his attitudes with the less attractive conduct of the English planters); it also belongs with a feminized dimension of Oroonoko's construction and an emphasis upon his constancy. But several factors undercut a romanticized delineation of Oroonoko's relationship with the narrator / governor's daughter. Chief among them is the fact that she is partly responsible for keeping Oroonoko in a state of perpetual enslavement, and this casts her opening self-presentation as a truth-teller, straight-talker and 'eye-witness' (p. 75) into doubt. Particularly destabilizing is the narrator's predilection for switching between the first and third person, and between the plural and singular personal. For example, when Oroonoko begins to agitate for his freedom, a plan is hatched whereby the white colonists will deploy delay tactics. Using the third person, Behn describes their actions: 'They fed him from day to day with promises, and delayed him . . . so that he began to suspect them of falsehood' (p. 113). Yet the subsequent paragraph problematizes the origins of the procedure, with the shift from the third person into the first person hinting at the narrator's own role in the conspiracy: 'I was obliged, by some persons, who feared a mutiny . . . to discourse with Caesar, and to give him all the satisfaction I possibly could' (p. 113), she explains. The unstable place of the narrator in relation to Oroonoko rules out any easy alliance between the white woman and black male, and gestures to other allegiances and confederacies that compromise the presentation of the fiction's only cross-racial and cross-gender encounter.

In common with Othello, Oroonoko realizes too late that his loyalties should lie with his own people. The discovery is belatedly made, despite hard experience. The royal slave's tales of his youth image him in constant conflict with other black men, only to discover subsequently that the very same enemies, as prisoners-of-war, can become 'very dear' (p. 100). Conversely, Oroonoko's 'delight in the white nations, and, above all, men of parts and wit' (p. 101) invariably culminates in treachery and his own disillusionment. The pattern of this narrative trajectory notwithstanding, it is only when Oroonoko has been repeatedly diverted, and when he has endured years of slavery, that he puts to one side rhetorical bravura and uses his oratorical skills for a more revolutionary purpose. Summoning the male slaves, he speaks to them 'of the miseries, and ignominies of slavery' (p. 125) in terms which, interestingly, debar any suggestion of a special relationship with the plantation's Englishwomen:

> we are bought and sold like apes, or monkeys, to be the sport of women, fools and cowards, and the support of rogues, runagades, that have abandoned their own countries, for raping, murders, thefts and villainies ... shall we render obedience to such a degenerate race? ... Will you ... suffer the lash from such hands? (p. 125)

The speech gathers up and pushes to their furthest extent what have been up to now the prose fiction's brief and essentially glancing anti-slavery sentiments. (Most of these are centred upon a linguistic coupling of the enslaved status of Oroonoko, Imoinda and their unborn child with race-specific discourses of disgrace and shame.) The immediate result of Oroonoko's exhortation is an uprising; under his lead, the slaves escape, hotly pursued by a hastily assembled local militia.

It is thematically revealing that this episode unfolds directly after the account of the visit to the native village and the relation of its scarifying, mutilating procedures. Commentaries on alterations to the natural body shape constituted a crucial part of contemporary 'monstrous' discourses. In 1653, for instance, John Bulwer wrote disapprovingly of the practice, among 'Indians', of 'deforming' by splicing the nose and of introducing 'artificial scars' in the form of 'carbonadoed faces', thus assuming the guise of 'monsters' and 'beasts'.[12] But Behn's fictional reading of such 'monsterizing' actions stages a significant departure from the scenario Bulwer envisages. For, in *Oroonoko*, the metaphorical freakshow is lent an unexpected twist. On this occasion, rather than Oroonoko or the 'rarities' of Surinam being placed on display, it is the English themselves who are exhibited. The logic underpinning the demonstration of extraordinary things is inverted, with 'wonder and amazement' (p. 121) at English strangeness and eccentricity being privileged as the Indians' responses. This shift in perspective exteriorizes the English party in such as way as to defamiliarize their appearance and point up the ludicrousness of their attire:

> we were dressed, so as is most commode for the hot countries, very glittering and rich . . . My own hair was cut short, and I had a taffeta cap, with black feathers, on my head. My brother was in a stuff suit, with silver loops and buttons, and abundance of green ribbon. This was all infinitely surprising to them . . . from gazing upon us round, they touched us, laying their hands upon all the features of our faces, feeling our breasts and arms, taking up one petticoat, then wondering to see another, admiring our shoes and stockings, but more our garters . . . (p. 121)

The abrupt reversal of the narrative gaze makes a striking impression. At once it dissolves that structure of racialized categories that keep separate white and black; more tellingly, it continues in the vein of earlier suggestions, hinting that barbarity and otherness cannot be contained within a single taxonomy. Although the gaze soon switches back, reinstating itself in the description of the spectacle of the Indian warlords' disfigured faces, it is nevertheless the English who, for a moment, are positioned as 'curiosities' on centre-stage. As a result, *Oroonoko* briefly displaces the colonial concentrations of its narrative and asks uncomfortable questions about the 'naturalized' location of human attributes.

No less destabilizing for a reader is the triumphant climax of Oroonoko's anti-slavery speech. The inspiring peroration is eventually revealed, not as an emancipatory blow against the institution of slavery, but as yet another misrecognition on Oroonoko's part: once again, he puts faith in the wrong place. Pursued by the army, the slaves desert Oroonoko one by one until only he, the heavily pregnant Imoinda and a third slave, the steadfast Tuscan, remain in the chase. When the previously loyal slaves take turns to whip Oroonoko during his public flogging at the militia's hands, a forceful suggestion of their unworthiness, and his ill-judged support, is driven home. Finally, even Tuscan is reconciled to the evil Byam: the slave's betrayal of his former leader is reflected in his key place in the second search party, which is organized when Oroonoko, once again, is believed to have deserted. The royal slave himself is left cogitating upon his primary error of having endeavoured 'to make those free, who were by nature slaves' (p. 130). Despite his stirring oratory and his knack for inspiring a revolution, Oroonoko is finally pictured as caught in an imprisoning ideological impasse.

The abolitionist argument was to become the central concern when *Oroonoko* was later reinvented for the stage, most notably by Thomas Southerne at the end of the century. No doubt in part because of this theatrical appropriation, Behn has received numerous critical plaudits and has been credited with producing an anti-slavery tract. In fact, as the foregoing discussion has shown, slavery, for Behn, is not the major preoccupation. Although the narrator makes clear her disapproval of the corrupt and tyrannous overseer who executes Oroonoko, it is Byam's individual actions, rather than the system itself, that appear intolerable. Moreover, Byam's Irishness is used to mark his distance from the other plantation owners. Indeed, we are left with the model of a well-run plantation, that of Colonel Martin, who resists the governor's offer of a final freakish demonstration. He refuses to exhibit the quartered body of Oroonoko, sent to him for display purposes, answering 'that he could govern his Negroes without terrifying and grieving them with frightful spectacles of a mangled king' (p. 140). At this point in the fiction, at least, *Oroonoko* seems poised between antithetical types of white authority.

In keeping with its broader about-turns and inconsistencies, however, *Oroonoko* does offer its readership one final 'monstrous' show, the sight of the protagonist being burned alive:

> he desired they would give him a pipe in his mouth, ready lighted
> ... and the executioner ... first cut off his members, and threw
> them into the fire. After that, with an ill-favoured knife, they cut

his ears, and his nose, and burned them; he still smoked on, as if nothing had touched him. Then they hacked off one of his arms, and still he bore up, and held his pipe. But at the cutting off the other arm, his head sunk, and his pipe dropped, and he gave up the ghost, without a groan, or a reproach.   (p. 140)

The grotesque demonstration concatenates many of *Oroonoko*'s considerations. At once, the passage invokes a freakshow experience, revealing to us both mutilation and visual horror, although here the dismemberment is visited upon Oroonoko and the spectacle is not of his own devising. With the narrator, we look upon the scene of the protagonist's demise and are thereby located, uncomfortably, in the role of paying, 'curious' customers. Further freakshow elements inhere in the association of Oroonoko with hellfire and devilry, and in the representation of the removal of his sexual parts, suggesting that the prince is elaborated in terms of a dangerous blackness and perceived according to a white logic of potentially unstable sexuality. Yet such racial stigmatization is simultaneously opened out to critique. The reduction of Oroonoko's body recalls the larger cultural dynamic of the belittlement and displacement of African peoples by the slave-trade, while the detail of giving 'up the ghost' points to possibilities of Christian redemption. Oroonoko, then, is still subject to a double-edged perspective: in performing in death a number of cultural practices, he reveals a mixed identity, which is neither African nor European but a mass of discordant elements. In so doing, he might be seen to stand in an analogous position to the seventeenth-century woman writer, herself a creative manifestation of opposites, herself productively uncertain of her ultimate ideological affiliations.

Notes

INTRODUCTION

1. Patricia Crawford, 'Women's published writings 1600–1700', in Mary Prior (ed.), *Women in English Society 1500–1800* (London and New York: Methuen, 1985), 211–82.
2. On such a bias in feminist literary history, see Margaret J. M. Ezell, *Writing Women's Literary History* (Baltimore and London: Johns Hopkins University Press, 1993), 39–65.

CHAPTER 1. DRAMA

1. Ros Ballaster, 'The first female dramatists', in Helen Wilcox (ed.), *Women and Literature in Britain, 1500–1700* (Cambridge: Cambridge University Press, 1996), 267.
2. Karen Raber, *Dramatic Difference: Gender, Class, and Genre in the Early Modern Closet Drama* (Newark: University of Delaware Press, 2001), 214.
3. Alison Findlay and Stephanie Hodgson-Wright, *Women and Dramatic Production 1550–1700* (Harlow: Longman, 2000), 11.
4. W. R. Owens and Lizbeth Goodman (eds), *Approaching Literature: Shakespeare, Aphra Behn and the Canon* (London: Routledge, 1996), 147.
5. *The Tragedy of Mariam*, in S. P. Cerasano and Marion Wynne-Davies (eds), *Renaissance Drama by Women: Texts and Documents* (London and New York: Routledge, 1996), Act I, lines 1–2, 5–7. Cited by act and line number hereafter in the text.
6. Margaret W. Ferguson, 'The Spectre of Resistance: *The Tragedy of Mariam*', in S. P. Cerasano and Marion Wynne-Davies (eds), *Readings in Renaissance Women's Drama: Criticism, History, and*

Performance 1594–1998 (London and New York: Routledge, 1998), 189.

7. Ibid.

8. Diane Purkiss (ed.), *Renaissance Women: The Plays of Elizabeth Cary / The Poems of Aemilia Lanyer* (London: Pickering, 1994), xx.

9. Dympna Callaghan, 'Re-Reading Elizabeth Cary's *The Tragedie of Mariam, Faire Queene of Jewry*', in Margo Hendricks and Patricia Parker (eds), *Women, 'Race', and Writing in the Early Modern Period* (London and New York: Routledge, 1994), 164.

CHAPTER 2. POETRY

1. Germaine Greer, Susan Hastings, Jeslyn Medoff and Melinda Sansone (eds), *Kissing the Rod: An Anthology of Seventeenth-Century Women's Verse* (London: Virago, 1988). Cited as *KR* hereafter in the text.

2. Jane Stevenson and Peter Davidson (eds), *Early Modern Women Poets (1520–1700): An Anthology* (Oxford: Oxford University Press, 2001).

3. Diane Purkiss (ed.), *Renaissance Women: The Plays of Elizabeth Cary/The Poems of Aemilia Lanyer* (London: Pickering, 1994). Cited by line number hereafter in the text.

4. See, for instance, Tina Krontiris, *Oppositional Voices: Women as Writers and Translators of Literature in the English Renaissance* (London and New York: Routledge, 1992).

5. Margaret J. M. Ezell, *Writing Women's Literary History* (Baltimore and London: Johns Hopkins University Press, 1993).

6. Stevenson and Davidson (eds), *Early Modern Women Poets*, xxx.

7. Mary Nyquist, 'Fallen Differences, Phallogocentric Discourses: Losing *Paradise Lost* to History', in Derek Attridge, Geoff Bennington and Robert Young (eds), *Post-Structuralism and the Question of History* (Cambridge: Cambridge University Press, 1987), 215.

8. Roland Barthes, *Image/Music/Text*, trans. Stephen Heath (London: Fontana, 1977), 165–9.

9. The commentary is extracted in Joan Larsen Klein (ed.), *Daughters, Wives and Widows: Writings by Men about Women and Marrriage in England, 1500–1640* (Urbana and Chicago: University of Illinois Press, 1992), 32.

10. John A. Philips, *Eve: The History of an Idea* (New York: Harper and Row, 1984), 135.

11. William Righter, *Myth and Literature* (London: Routledge, 1975), 104.

CHAPTER 3. MOTHERS' ADVICE BOOKS

1. Both texts are reprinted in Sylvia Brown (ed.), *Women's Writing in Stuart England: The Mothers' Legacies of Dorothy Leigh, Elizabeth Joscelin and Elizabeth Richardson* (Thrupp: Sutton, 1999). Cited as *WW* hereafter in the text.
2. Since the Sylvia Brown volume does not print the 1632 editorial matter, I have quoted from Elizabeth Joscelin, *The Mother's Legacy to Her Unborn Child*, ed. Lord Bishop of Rochester (London and New York: Macmillan, 1894), A10^r. Cited as Joscelin hereafter in the text.
3. Nicholas Breton, *The Mother's Blessing* (London, 1602; S.T.C. 3669); Elizabeth Grymeston, *Miscellanea. Meditations. Memoratives* (London, 1604; S.T.C. 12407). Cited as Grymeston hereafter in the text.
4. These are housed in the National Library of Scotland (MSS 6489 and 6492).
5. See Linda Pollock, *With Faith and Physic: The Life of a Tudor Gentlewoman, Lady Grace Mildmay (1552–1620)* (London: Collins & Brown, 1993).
6. Kristen Poole, '"The fittest closet for all goodness": Authorial Strategies of Jacobean Mothers' Manuals', *Studies in English Literature*, 35 (1995), 69–88.
7. Linda Pollock, 'Embarking on a Rough Passage: The Experience of Pregnancy in Early Modern Society', in Valerie Fildes (ed.), *Women as Mothers in Pre-Industrial England* (London and New York: Routledge, 1990), 39–67.
8. Valerie Wayne, 'Advice for women from mothers and patriarchs', in Helen Wilcox (ed.), *Women and Literature in Britain 1500–1700* (Cambridge: Cambridge University Press, 1996), 64.

CHAPTER 4. PROPHECY

1. Patricia Crawford, 'Women's published writings 1600–1700', in Mary Prior (ed.), *Women in English Society 1500–1800* (London and New York: Methuen, 1985), 211–82.
2. Diane Purkiss, 'Producing the voice, consuming the body: Women prophets of the seventeenth century', in Isobel Grundy and Susan Wiseman (eds), *Women, Writing, History 1640–1740* (London: Batsford, 1992), 139.
3. Elinor Channel, *A Message from God by a Dumb Woman* (London, 1653; Wing C1936), 1; Anna Trapnel, *The Cry of a Stone* (London, 1654; Wing T2031), 42. Cited as *CS* hereafter in the text.

4. Phyllis Mack, *Visionary Women: Ecstatic Prophecy in Seventeenth-Century England* (Berkeley: University of California Press, 1992), 15–44.

5. Sue Wiseman, 'Unsilent instruments and the devil's cushions: Authority in seventeenth-century women's prophetic discourse', in Isobel Armstrong (ed.), *New Feminist Discourses: Critical Essays on Theories and Texts* (London and New York: Routledge, 1992), 183.

6. Mary Cary, *The Little Horn's Doom* (London, 1651; Wing C736), A8^r.

7. Purkiss, 'Producing the voice', 140.

8. Anna Trapnel, *Anna Trapnel's Report* (London, 1654; Wing T2033), A2^r. Cited as *R.* hereafter in the text.

9. Peter Gaunt, *Oliver Cromwell* (Oxford: Blackwell, 1996), 232.

10. Elspeth Graham, Hilary Hinds, Elaine Hobby and Helen Wilcox (eds), *Her Own Life: Autobiographical Writings by Seventeenth-Century Englishwomen* (London and New York: Routledge, 1989), 73.

11. Ibid.

CHAPTER 5. DIARIES AND MEMOIRS

1. *Diary of Lady Margaret Hoby, 1599–1605*, ed. Dorothy M. Meads (London: Routledge, 1930), 93.

2. Ibid.

3. Samuel Bury, *An Account of the Life and Death of Mrs Elizabeth Bury* (Bristol: J. Penn, 1720), 9–10.

4. Sara Heller Mendelson, 'Stuart women's diaries and occasional memoirs', in Mary Prior (ed.), *Women in English Society 1500–1800* (London and New York: Methuen, 1985), 185.

5. Elspeth Graham, Hilary Hinds, Elaine Hobby and Helen Wilcox (eds), *Her Own Life: Autobiographical Writings by Seventeenth-Century Englishwomen* (London and New York: Routledge, 1989), 97.

6. Alice Thornton, *The Autobiography of Mrs Alice Thornton of East Newton, Co. York*, ed. Charles Jackson, Surtees Society, 62 (1873), 1.

7. *The Memoirs of Anne, Lady Halkett and Ann, Lady Fanshawe*, ed. John Loftis (Oxford: Clarendon, 1979), 101.

8. Theodosia Alleine, *The Life and Death of Mr Joseph Alleine* (London, 1671; Wing A1011), 46.

9. Lucy Hutchinson, *Memoirs of the Life of Colonel Hutchinson*, ed. James Sutherland (Oxford: Oxford University Press, 1973), 110–14.

10. *The Memoirs*, ed. Loftis, 239–41.
11. Edward W. Said, *Orientalism* (New York: Random House, 1979), 21.
12. Mary Rich, *Autobiography of Mary, Countess of Warwick*, ed. T. Croker (London: Percy Society, 1848); Mary Rich, *Memoir of Lady Warwick: Also her Diary* (London: English Monthly Tract Society, 1847). Cited as either *A.* or *M.* hereafter in the text. Because the English Monthly Tract Society edition is incomplete (it prints only part of Rich's original manuscript), I have also consulted works which include some of the *Diary*'s missing sections.
13. Jacqueline Pearson, 'Women reading, reading women', in Helen Wilcox (ed.), *Women and Literature in Britain 1500–1700* (Cambridge: Cambridge University Press, 1996), 80–99.
14. Ralph Houlbrooke (ed.), *English Family Life, 1576–1716: An Anthology from Diaries* (Oxford: Blackwell, 1988), 80.

CHAPTER 6. CONVERSION NARRATIVES

1. Hannah Allen, *Satan His Methods and Malice Baffled* (London, 1683; Wing A1025), 18. Cited as *S.* hereafter in the text.
2. Edmund Calamy, *The Godly Man's Ark* (London, 1657; Wing C247); Sarah Davy, *Heaven Realized* (London, 1670; Wing D444).
3. Davy, *Heaven Realized*, B7^v.
4. Ibid., A5^v.
5. Jane Turner, *Choice Experiences* (London, 1653; Wing T3294), B4^{r-v}.
6. Ibid., A2^r–B7^r.
7. Elspeth Graham, Hilary Hinds, Elaine Hobby and Helen Wilcox (eds), *Her Own Life: Autobiographical Writings by Seventeenth-Century Englishwomen* (London and New York: Routledge, 1989), 199. The narratives appear on pp. 165–79, 197–210, 211–24.
8. Elspeth Graham, 'Women's writing and the self', in Helen Wilcox (ed.), *Women and Literature in Britain 1500–1700* (Cambridge: Cambridge University Press, 1996), 219.
9. Pashur, the son of a priest, is described in Jeremiah 20:1–4 as a 'Magor Missabib' or, literally, 'a terror to thyself, and to all thy friends'.
10. See Sandra Cavallo and Lyndan Warner (eds), *Widowhood in Medieval and Early Modern Europe* (Harlow: Longman, 1999), *passim*.
11. Barbara J. Todd, 'The Virtuous Widow in Protestant England', in Cavallo and Warner (eds), *Widowhood in Medieval and Early Modern Europe*, 73.

CHAPTER 7. PROSE FICTION

1. Moira Ferguson (ed.), *First Feminists: British Women Writers, 1578–1799* (Bloomington: Indiana University Press, 1985), 56.
2. Mary Ellen Lamb, 'The Biopolitics of Romance in Mary Wroth's *The Countess of Montgomery's Urania'*, *English Literary Renaissance*, 31 (2001), 107.
3. Paul Salzman (ed.), *An Anthology of Seventeenth-Century Fiction* (Oxford: Oxford University Press, 1991), 203.
4. Denny's verse and Wroth's reply are printed in Josephine A. Roberts, 'An Unpublished Literary Quarrel Concerning the Suppression of Mary Wroth's *Urania'*, *Notes and Queries*, 222 (1977), 532–5.
5. Margaret Cavendish, *'The Blazing World' and Other Writings*, ed. Kate Lilly (Harmondsworth: Penguin, 1992), xii.
6. Helen Hackett, *Women and Romance Fiction in the English Renaissance* (Cambridge: Cambridge University Press, 2000), 188.
7. Janet Todd, *The Sign of Angellica: Women, Writing, and Fiction, 1660–1800* (London: Virago, 1989), 80.
8. Aphra Behn, *'Oroonoko', 'The Rover' and Other Works*, ed. Janet Todd (Harmondsworth: Penguin, 1992), 75. Cited by page number hereafter in the text.
9. Mark Thornton Burnett, *Constructing 'Monsters' in Shakespearean Drama and Early Modern Culture* (Basingstoke: Palgrave, 2002), 12.
10. Barbara Maria Stafford, *Body Criticism: Imaging the Unseen in Enlightenment Art and Medicine* (Cambridge, MA: MIT Press, 1991), 319.
11. A variation on *buckra* or *bakra* (master), the term used by Surinam natives for the whites.
12. John Bulwer, *Anthropometamorphosis* (London, 1653; Wing B5461), 119, 163, 247.

Select Bibliography

PRIMARY WORKS BY SEVENTEENTH-CENTURY WOMEN WRITERS

Alleine, Theodosia, *The Life and Death of Mr Joseph Alleine* (London, 1671; Wing A1011).

Allen, Hannah, *Satan His Methods and Malice Baffled* (London, 1683; Wing A1025).

Behn, Aphra, *'Oroonoko', 'The Rover' and Other Works*, ed. Janet Todd (Harmondsworth: Penguin, 1992).

Brown, Sylvia (ed.), *Women's Writing in Stuart England: The Mothers' Legacies of Dorothy Leigh, Elizabeth Joscelin and Elizabeth Richardson* (Thrupp: Sutton, 1999). A highly readable and scholarly anthology.

Calamy, Edmund, *The Godly Man's Ark* (London, 1657; Wing C247). This compilation features a number of religious narratives by seventeenth-century women.

Cary, Elizabeth, *The Tragedy of Mariam* (1613), in S. P. Cerasano and Marion Wynne-Davies (eds), *Renaissance Drama by Women: Texts and Documents* (London and New York: Routledge, 1996), 43–75. A fine collection of plays by early modern women.

Cary, Mary, *The Little Horn's Doom* (London, 1651; Wing C736).

Cavendish, Margaret, *'The Blazing World' and Other Writings*, ed. Kate Lilly (Harmondsworth: Penguin, 1992).

Channel, Elinor, *A Message from God by a Dumb Woman* (London, 1653; Wing C1936).

Davy, Sarah, *Heaven Realized* (London, 1670; Wing D444).

Ferguson, Moira (ed.), *First Feminists: British Women Writers, 1578–1799* (Bloomington: Indiana University Press, 1985). A facilitating collection of extracts from sixteenth-, seventeenth- and eighteenth-century women writers.

Graham, Elspeth, Hilary Hinds, Elaine Hobby and Helen Wilcox (eds), *Her Own Life: Autobiographical Writings by Seventeenth-Century*

Englishwomen (London and New York: Routledge, 1989). An excellent compilation of seventeenth-century women's autobiographies.

Greer, Germaine, Susan Hastings, Jeslyn Medoff and Melinda Sansone (eds), *Kissing the Rod: An Anthology of Seventeenth-Century Women's Verse* (London: Virago, 1988). The standard selection of poetry by seventeenth-century women.

Grymeston, Elizabeth, *Miscellanea. Meditations. Memoratives* (London, 1604; S.T.C. 12407).

Halkett, Lady Anne, 'Mother's Will to Her Unborn Child' (1656) and 'To My Son, Robert Halkett' (1670). National Library of Scotland (MSS 6489 and 6492).

Hoby, Margaret, *Diary of Lady Margaret Hoby, 1599–1605*, ed. Dorothy M. Meads (London: Routledge, 1930).

Houlbrooke, Ralph (ed.), *English Family Life, 1576–1716: An Anthology from Diaries* (Oxford: Blackwell, 1988). This collection includes (pp. 80–87) an alternative selection from the diary of Mary Rich, Countess of Warwick.

Hutchinson, Lucy, *Memoirs of the Life of Colonel Hutchinson*, ed. James Sutherland (Oxford: Oxford University Press, 1973).

Joscelin, Elizabeth, *The Mother's Legacy to Her Unborn Child*, ed. Lord Bishop of Rochester (London and New York: Macmillan, 1894). Reproduces the 1632 edition of Joscelin's legacy.

Loftis, John (ed.), *The Memoirs of Anne, Lady Halkett and Ann, Lady Fanshawe* (Oxford: Clarendon Press, 1979).

Purkiss, Diane (ed.), *Renaissance Women: The Plays of Elizabeth Cary / The Poems of Aemilia Lanyer* (London: Pickering, 1994).

Rich, Mary, *Autobiography of Mary, Countess of Warwick*, ed. T. Croker (London: Percy Society, 1848).

—— *Memoir of Lady Warwick: Also her Diary* (London: English Monthly Tract Society, 1847).

Stevenson, Jane, and Peter Davidson (eds), *Early Modern Women Poets (1520–1700): An Anthology* (Oxford: Oxford University Press, 2001). This edition offers a full sense of the social and cultural range of poetic writing by early modern women.

Thornton, Alice, *The Autobiography of Mrs Alice Thornton of East Newton, Co. York*, ed. Charles Jackson, Surtees Society, 62 (1873).

Trapnel, Anna, *Anna Trapnel's Report* (London, 1654; Wing T2033).

—— *The Cry of a Stone* (London, 1654; Wing T203).

Turner, Jane, *Choice Experiences* (London, 1653; Wing T3294).

Wroth, Lady Mary, *Urania*, in Paul Salzman (ed.), *An Anthology of Seventeenth-Century Fiction* (Oxford: Oxford University Press, 1991), 3–208.

PRIMARY WORKS ABOUT SEVENTEENTH-CENTURY WOMEN

Breton, Nicholas, *The Mother's Blessing* (London, 1602; S.T.C. 3669).

Bulwer, John, *Anthropometamorphosis* (London, 1653; Wing B5461).

Bury, Samuel, *An Account of the Life and Death of Mrs Elizabeth Bury* (Bristol: J. Penn, 1720).

Klein, Joan Larsen (ed.), *Daughters, Wives and Widows: Writings by Men about Women and Marrriage in England, 1500–1640* (Urbana and Chicago: University of Illinois Press, 1992). A useful introduction to the range of masculine opinion about women in early modern England.

CRITICAL AND BIOGRAPHICAL STUDIES

Ballaster, Ros, 'The first female dramatists', in Helen Wilcox (ed.), *Women and Literature in Britain, 1500–1700* (Cambridge: Cambridge University Press, 1996), 267–90. All of the essays in this anthology represent original and articulate contributions.

Barthes, Roland, *Image/Music/Text*, trans. Stephen Heath (London: Fontana, 1977).

Burnett, Mark Thornton, *Constructing 'Monsters' in Shakespearean Drama and Early Modern Culture* (Basingstoke: Palgrave, 2002).

Callaghan, Dympna, 'Re-Reading Elizabeth Cary's *The Tragedie of Mariam, Faire Queene of Jewry*', in Margo Hendricks and Patricia Parker (eds), *Women, 'Race', and Writing in the Early Modern Period* (London and New York: Routledge, 1994), 163–77.

Cavallo, Sandra, and Lyndan Warner (eds), *Widowhood in Medieval and Early Modern Europe* (Harlow: Longman, 1999).

Crawford, Patricia, 'Women's published writings 1600–1700', in Mary Prior (ed.), *Women in English Society 1500–1800* (London and New York: Methuen, 1985), 211–82. The essays in this collection offer a sound historical guide to women in the period.

Ezell, Margaret J. M., *Writing Women's Literary History* (Baltimore and London: Johns Hopkins University Press, 1993).

Ferguson, Margaret W., 'The Spectre of Resistance: *The Tragedy of Mariam*', in S. P. Cerasano and Marion Wynne-Davies (eds), *Readings in Renaissance Women's Drama: Criticism, History, and Performance 1594–1998* (London and New York: Routledge, 1998), 182–93. The anthology is essential reading for those interested in seventeenth-century women's drama.

Findlay, Alison, and Stephanie Hodgson-Wright with Gweno Williams, *Women and Dramatic Production 1550–1700* (Harlow: Longman, 2000).

Gaunt, Peter, *Oliver Cromwell* (Oxford: Blackwell, 1996).

Graham, Elspeth, 'Women's writing and the self', in Helen Wilcox (ed.), *Women and Literature in Britain 1500–1700* (Cambridge: Cambridge University Press, 1996), 209–34.

Hackett, Helen, *Women and Romance Fiction in the English Renaissance* (Cambridge: Cambridge University Press, 2000).

Krontiris, Tina, *Oppositional Voices: Women as Writers and Translators of Literature in the English Renaissance* (London and New York: Routledge, 1992).

Lamb, Mary Ellen, 'The Biopolitics of Romance in Mary Wroth's *The Countess of Montgomery's Urania*', *English Literary Renaissance*, 31 (2001), 107–30.

Mack, Phyllis, *Visionary Women: Ecstatic Prophecy in Seventeenth-Century England* (Berkeley: University of California Press, 1992).

Mendelson, Sara Heller, 'Stuart women's diaries and occasional memoirs', in Mary Prior (ed.), *Women in English Society 1500–1800* (London and New York: Methuen, 1985), 181–201.

Nyquist, Mary, 'Fallen Differences, Phallogocentric Discourses: Losing *Paradise Lost* to History', in Derek Attridge, Geoff Bennington and Robert Young (eds), *Post-Structuralism and the Question of History* (Cambridge: Cambridge University Press, 1987), 212–43.

Owens, W. R., and Lizbeth Goodman (eds), *Approaching Literature: Shakespeare, Aphra Behn and the Canon* (London: Routledge, 1996).

Pearson, Jacqueline, 'Women reading, reading women', in Helen Wilcox (ed.), *Women and Literature in Britain 1500–1700* (Cambridge: Cambridge University Press, 1996), 80–99.

Philips, John A., *Eve: The History of an Idea* (New York: Harper and Row, 1984).

Pollock, Linda, 'Embarking on a Rough Passage: The Experience of Pregnancy in Early Modern Society', in Valerie Fildes (ed.), *Women as Mothers in Pre-Industrial England* (London and New York: Routledge, 1990), 39–67.

—— *With Faith and Physic: The Life of a Tudor Gentlewoman, Lady Grace Mildmay (1552–1620)* (London: Collins & Brown, 1993).

Poole, Kristen, ' "The fittest closet for all goodness": Authorial Strategies of Jacobean Mothers' Manuals', *Studies in English Literature*, 35 (1995), 69–88.

Purkiss, Diane, 'Producing the voice, consuming the body: Women prophets of the seventeenth century', in Isobel Grundy and Susan Wiseman (eds), *Women, Writing, History 1640–1740* (London: Batsford, 1992), 139–58. A collection of groundbreaking discussions.

Raber, Karen, *Dramatic Difference: Gender, Class, and Genre in the Early Modern Closet Drama* (Newark: University of Delaware Press, 2001).

Righter, William, *Myth and Literature* (London: Routledge, 1975).

Roberts, Josephine A., 'An Unpublished Literary Quarrel Concerning the Suppression of Mary Wroth's *Urania*', *Notes and Queries*, 222 (1977), 532–5.

Said, Edward W., *Orientalism* (New York: Random House, 1979).

Stafford, Barbara Maria, *Body Criticism: Imaging the Unseen in Enlightenment Art and Medicine* (Cambridge, MA: MIT Press, 1991).

Todd, Barbara J., 'The Virtuous Widow in Protestant England', in Sandra Cavallo and Lyndan Warner (eds), *Widowhood in Medieval and Early Modern Europe* (Harlow: Longman, 1999), 66–83.

Todd, Janet, *The Sign of Angellica: Women, Writing, and Fiction, 1660–1800* (London: Virago, 1989). A vital study which was among the first to recover the importance of seventeenth-century women's writing.

Wayne, Valerie, 'Advice for women from mothers and patriarchs', in Helen Wilcox (ed.), *Women and Literature in Britain 1500–1700* (Cambridge: Cambridge University Press, 1996), 56–79.

Wiseman, Sue, 'Unsilent instruments and the devil's cushions: Authority in seventeenth-century women's prophetic discourse', in Isobel Armstrong (ed.), *New Feminist Discourses: Critical Essays on Theories and Texts* (London and New York: Routledge, 1992), 176–96.

BACKGROUND READING OR OTHER RELEVANT WORKS

Apart from the items listed above, readers may wish to consult the following:

Battigelli, Anna, *Margaret Cavendish and the Exiles of the Mind* (Lexington: University Press of Kentucky, 1998). A lively study of Cavendish's scientific preoccupations.

Beilin, Elaine V., *Redeeming Eve: Women Writers of the English Renaissance* (Princeton: Princeton University Press, 1987). Contains pertinent chapters on Lanyer, mothers' advice books and Wroth.

Brant, Clare, and Diane Purkiss (eds), *Women, Texts and Histories, 1575–1760* (London and New York: Routledge, 1992). A wide-ranging and important anthology.

Burke, Mary, Jane Donawerth, Linda L. Dove and Karen Nelson (eds), *Women, Writing, and the Reproduction of Culture in Tudor and Stuart Britain* (Syracuse: Syracuse University Press, 2000). A nuanced collection on early modern women's writing that draws upon feminist cultural studies.

Chedgzoy, Kate, Melanie Hansen and Suzanne Trill (eds), *Voicing Women: Gender and Sexuality in Early Modern Writing* (Keele: Keele University Press, 1996). As well as offering fresh, theoretically inspired readings of women writers, this collection brings new material to light.

Clarke, Daniel, and Elizabeth Clarke (eds), *'This Double Voice': Gendered Writing in Early Modern England* (Basingstoke: Macmillan, 2000). Historically and theoretically grounded discussions of 'difference'.

Daybell, James (ed.), *Early Modern Women's Letter Writing, 1450–1700* (Basingstoke: Palgrave, 2001). This landmark book of essays examines the development of women's letter writing from the late fifteenth to the early eighteenth centuries.

Donovan, Josephine, *Women and the Rise of the Novel, 1405–1726* (New York: St Martin's, 2000). A clear and informative account.

Grossman, Marshall (ed.), *Aemilia Lanyer: Gender, Genre and the Canon* (Lexington: University Press of Kentucky, 1998). Uses the poetry of Lanyer to interrogate that of her male contemporaries.

Haselkorn, Anne M., and Betty S. Travitsky (eds), *The Renaissance Englishwoman in Print: Counterbalancing the Canon* (Amherst: University of Massachusetts Press, 1990). An exciting revisionist collection.

Hinds, Hilary, *God's Englishwomen: Seventeenth-Century Radical Sectarian Writing and Feminist Criticism* (Manchester: Manchester University Press, 1996). Investigates the writings of women in the radical sects of the seventeenth century through the lens of feminist literary criticism.

Hobby, Elaine, *Virtue of Necessity: English Women's Writing, 1649–1688* (London: Virago, 1988). A leader in the field.

Lamb, Mary Ellen, *Gender and Authorship in the Sidney Circle* (Madison: University of Wisconsin Press, 1990). Highly readable account of the literary connections between the male and female members of the Sidney and Herbert families.

Lewalski, Barbara Kiefer, *Writing Women in Jacobean England* (Cambridge, MA: Harvard University Press, 1993). A magisterial volume.

Pacheco, Anita (ed.), *Early Women Writers, 1600–1720* (London and New York: Longman, 1998). A helpful collection of classic articles and essays.

Rubik, Margarete, *Early Women Dramatists, 1550–1800* (Basingstoke: Macmillan, 1998). Full of detail and insight.

Smith, Barbara, and Ursula Appelt (eds), *Write and Be Written: Early Modern Women Poets and Cultural Constraints* (Aldershot: Ashgate,

2001). The essays featured apply new critical methodologies and theories to a reassessment of early modern women poets.

Woods, Susanne, *Lanyer: A Renaissance Woman Poet* (Oxford: Oxford University Press, 1999). The standard critical biography.

Index